The Sunfish Book

Will
White

The Sunfish
Book

Hearst Marine Books
New York

Manufactured in the United States of America.
Designed by Design & Devices, Inc.

Library of Congress Cataloging in Publication Data

White, Will W., 1932–
    The sunfish book.

    Includes index.
    1. Sunfish (Sailboats) 2. Sailing. I. Title.
GV811.63.S94W44   1982   797.1′24 82–10414

ISBN 0-914814–31–1

● **Dedication**
To all the wives and children, boyfriends and
girlfriends who follow the Sunfish regatta
circuit, especially to my own camp followers,
and especially to Elizabeth, this book is dedi-
cated. Without them there would have been no
book.

Acknowledgments

Sailors everywhere seem to delight in talking about their sport and telling you, without reservation, why they think they are fast. I owe all those who spoke with me a big debt of thanks, from Carl Knight, the old master, to Dave Chapin, the World Sunfish Champion in 1979 and 1981 and the *Yacht Racing/Cruising* 1980 Dinghy Sailor of the Year.

Others whose brains I've picked include Gerrit Zeestraten, formerly of Curaçao (I'd like to see him race Dave Chapin in trade wind conditions.), Paul Fendler, and the champions I interviewed for this book. I want particularly to acknowledge Paul Odegard and Derrick Fries, two of the most consistent sailors in the class and two of the most astute students of the boat itself. Both had books brewing in the backs of their minds and both bore off when they learned I had a head start on them.

I would like to thank those at Alcort who were so helpful: Bruce Connolly, John Ray—original editor of *Scuttlebut*, the first Sunfish newsletter—Jack Evans, Warren Bowes, Rick Wonson, Bob Johnstone—who made a knockout movie called *Sail to Freedom* that really captures the magic of the Sunfish—Eric Skemp and Steve Baker.

I have to thank all the old-timers at the Darien (Connecticut) Sunfish Yacht Racing Association, whose sailors dominated the class in the mid-60s, and the Barrington (Rhode Island) Frostbite Racing Association, which has helped develop at least three of the most recent North American champions.

Much of the book was dictated while I traveled to and from regattas. I'd like to thank Jeannie Marshall, one of the world's nicest people and a magician on the IBM System 6 Word Processor.

Acknowledgments 7
Introduction 10

1. **Background to the Boat**. 12
   Class Development
   The Sail
   The Daggerboard
   Mast and Rigging
   Eyebolt
   Super Sunfish

2. **Ashore and Afloat** 32
   Transportation
   From Shore to Water
   Launching from the Beach
   Launching from a Dock
   How to Sit in a Sunfish
   Safety on the Water
   Staying Upright in Heavy Wind
   Clothing

3. **Tuning the Boat** 44
   The Rudder
   The Daggerboard
   The Bridle
   The Cockpit
   Sheet Blocks
   The Foredeck
   The Compass
   Other Stuff on the Foredeck
   The Hull

4. **Tuning the Rig** 58
The Gooseneck
The Jens Rig
Bending on the Sail
The Free End of the Halyard
Telltales

5. **Tuning You** 66
Hiking Muscles
Sheeting Muscles
Pads
Shoes
Carrying Weight

6. **The Start and the Windward Leg** 70
The Start
The Windward Leg
Lifts and Headers
Tacking
Windward Tactics
The Windward Mark

7. **Off the Wind** 100
Reach Speed
Reach Tactics
Rounding the Leeward Mark—1
The Second Windward Leg
The Leeward or Downwind Leg
Rounding the Leeward Mark—2
The Last Beat

8. **The Finish** 122
Windward Finishes
Downwind Finishes
After the Race

9. **Interviews with the Champions** 126
Mike Catalano
Dave Chapin
Derrick Fries
Joel Furman
Paul Odegard
Nat Philbrick
Cor van Aanholt

10. **River Racing** 164

11. **The Cruising Sunfish** 170

9

Will White at the 1977 National Team Race Championship in Bristol, Rhode Island. The sail was an experimental version built by Ratsey.

● Introduction

The Sunfish is pure sailing, the essence of sailing. Practically no upkeep. No worries about moorings and boat yards. Five minutes from arriving at the water's edge, you can be off and sailing. It was the first off-the-beach boat and it introduced thousands of people to the sport.

The Sunfish was designed with no preconceptions. It is doubtful that a naval architect, thoroughly indoctrinated in fine bow entries for speed to windward and high-aspect-ratio marconi sails for aerodynamic efficiency, would have come up with a mackerel's-head-and-cod's-tail hull, or the absurd equilateral triangle sail. But these two features are among those that give the Sunfish its character.

The shallow vee-bottom of the hull, together with its rather generous beam, or width, makes the Sunfish comparatively stable and forgiving. It's an ideal boat for children or those learning to sail. It can be righted easily if it capsizes. Most small sailboats capsize quite regularly. But a Sunfish was the first one you could right, climb back aboard, and sail off without worrying about whether you could get the water out before you capsized again. In fact, it is quite possible to anticipate the capsize, roll over on the daggerboard as the mast hits the water, pop it back upright with the same rolling motion, and hardly get your socks wet.

The crazy lateen rig is another benefit. Drop the sail, lift out the mast, and roll everything together in one simple package the same length as the boat. While others are still fussing with sleeves and tracks, multisection masts and booms, and sail battens, you are on the road home or relaxing on the beach.

Just as the Sunfish represents pure sailing, it offers pure sailboat racing. No need for a new set of sails every year. Your one triangular sail, properly set on the spars, will last for years and still be competitive. No need to keep buying or changing expensive hardware to keep up with the latest sailing theory. Even if you attach the best of everything allowed by the class rules, you'll have a hard time spending more than $100.

It is important to know something about the people who race Sunfish, too. Each major racing class has a personality of its own, and I think the Sunfish crowd has a very special mystique. They are not particularly clannish and they are happy to welcome new people. They tend to be family-oriented, and attend regattas with wives and/or husbands and children. The racing tends to be fierce, but joyfully so, and the abrasions are usually left out on the water. Most of the young champions grew up with Sunfish, learning to sail from their parents or older siblings, who may have been champions in their day. Each new regatta is like a family reunion. So if you want competition with a sense of fun, Sunfish racing is probably for you.

Your Sunfish should remain competitive for a lifetime, if properly maintained. It is, by some people's reckoning, overbuilt. It can withstand abuse that would crack most racing dinghies like an egg shell. Of course, nothing in this world is perfect. The Sunfish is mass produced and occasionally a lemon will slip by. This almost always takes the form of a leaker,

exceedingly annoying but usually easy to fix with a little resin and filler. Another flaw I find a little maddening in an otherwise well-made boat is the finish on the wood parts. Of course, fine varnished mahogany is almost as rare in small boat building today as silver-plated hardware, so perhaps I am overcritical. Otherwise, the Sunfish is a yacht-quality boat.

In all, I must admit I am crazy about the Sunfish. It is pure sailing, and sailing is the most fun you can have with your clothes on. (My apologies to Jerry DeLaFemina, a fellow toiler in the advertising vineyards, who thinks advertising fits that definition. Advertising sure is fun, but not as much fun as sailing!)

Will W. White
West Hartford, Connecticut

1 *Background to the Boat*

LIFE'S OUT STOP WE'RE IN STOP ALL'S FORGIVEN STOP COME HOME
Cortlandt Heyniger was on holiday in the Southwest when he got that telegram from his partner, Alex Bryan. It brought Cort home to Waterbury, Connecticut, by the next available means of transportation. The telegram referred to a spread in *Life* about a funny looking sailing machine called the Sailfish. It was August, 1948, and the fledgling firm of Alcort, Inc. was 2½ years old. (They named their company Alcort instead of Cortal so it would be up front in the Yellow Pages.)

Alex and Cort had been friends since they were in kindergarten together. "We were house builders at an early age," according to Alex. They formed the Prospect Street Hut Society, and rebuilt the hut several times. That was followed by a glider ("fortunately it didn't fly") and their first commercial venture, a gadget called the "Klickety-Klack-Marble-Track." They had no formal training in woodworking; "we simply taught each other."

"We were still in school, and we made some ice boats. That's what started the whole thing," Cort told me recently. They were basically Skeeter class sailboats, with 75 square feet of sail. Most Skeeters are one-man boats, but the partners built a one-design version that sat two and called it the Yankee class. It was mainly a venture for fun. "The winter before the war we only had one weekend we couldn't sail, and we never had so much fun in our lives," Cort said. It was 1941, and they did not return from war for four years. When they got home, they found that the barn in which their Skeeters were stored was burned to the ground, but fortunately the owner had insured the building's contents. They returned to a pile of ashes but there were also orders for more Skeeters. That was enough to put Alcort into business.

Cort again: "We made ice boats and then we needed something for the summertime. We tried row boats and we put together a few hobby kits, and then this fellow came in and wanted us to make a paddle board for the Red Cross. We told him how much it would cost. He threw up his hands and said the Red Cross couldn't afford it. But he made the mistake of leaving the plans there, which were not much, and we made one anyway. Alex put a canoe sail on it and that's what started the Sailfish.

"That was the first one. The thing was only 22 inches wide and we were trying to figure some way to keep it upright. Obviously we needed more beam, which we put on the next one. It was like trying to sail a log, that first one.

"We went through a couple more models. The first Sailfish was 14 feet and then we couldn't get any 14-foot plywood. So we made some 12-footers. That's the one that got into *Life*. That really was the first Sailfish—the 12-footer."

The first few dozen Sailfish were sold to friends on various small lakes around Connecticut and central Massachusetts, and on Long Island Sound. The Waterbury newspaper heard about it and wrote it up. At that point, they were still calling it the Sailboard. A marketing friend told them that "Sailboard" would never do. He had a Sailfish trophy mounted in his office, and somebody said, "That's it!" or "Eureka!" or something, and the Sailfish was christened.

The first plant was in the loft of a lumber yard, a two-story brick warehouse building. After the *Life* article, they outgrew the loft, and then two more buildings on the north end of Waterbury.

How did the *Life* article come about? A clever promotion man? "No," Cort says. "A friend of ours brought a date up from New York. She could sail the Sailfish better than he could, and she had never seen it before. It turned out she was one of the music editors for *Life*. She went back to New York and said, 'Hey, fellows, here's something that would make a good story.' We didn't know anything about it until they called up and wondered if we could get something together, and where. We suggested Madison, Connecticut.

"We went down there for the weekend, and Saturday we had about 15 boats there. We had a lot of friends and they helped us a lot. They came from all over Connecticut. The only trouble was, it rained Saturday and it was foggy all day Sunday, so we couldn't take any pictures. And there was no wind. The *Life* people went back to New York.

"On the next Monday, we got word from the weather department up in Hartford that it was going to be a good day. They had told us in New York, 'When you get some good weather going, we'll come back.'

"Alex had been in the Air Corps, and he knew about weather reports. So we told the

Al and Cort of Alcort, who parlayed a surfboard with a sail into the most popular racing sailboat and family fun boat in the world—the Sunfish. Alex "Red" Bryan on the left, with Cortlandt "Bud" Heyniger and a mess of Sunfish.

13

This is the way your Sunfish came if you bought it in the early '50s.

14

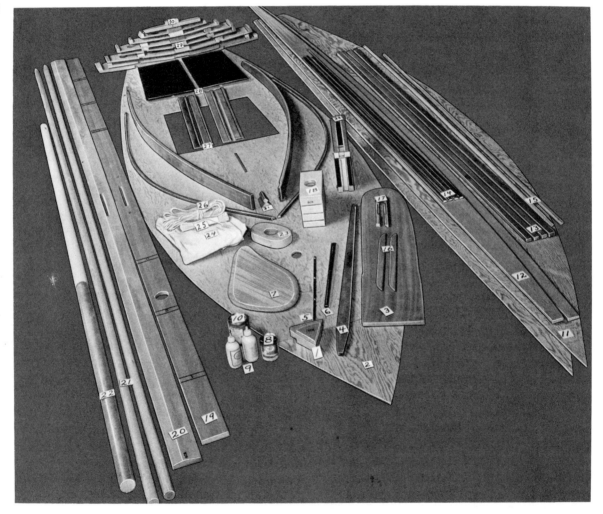

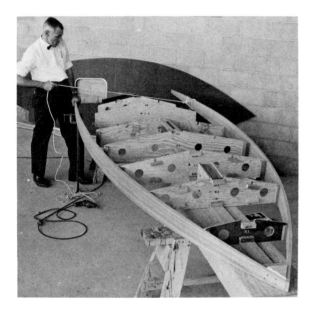

Cort Heyniger demonstrates how the topside strakes were bent to the ribs in building a Sunfish from a kit. Kits have not been marketed by Alcort since the mid-60s.

Life people to come back at noon on Monday, because that's when it was going to start.

"Well, they came up and took pictures all Monday afternoon and some on Tuesday. They went away, and later we called them, and they said, 'Well, we've got all these pictures and a story written up, but we don't know whether it will get in the magazine or not.'"

The story did appear, and a whole new kind of yachting was born.

Almost from the beginning, Alcort sold kits as well as finished boats. I asked Cort how long it would take an average handy person to build a Sailfish from a kit. "It said in the catalog a few dozen hours. The handier he is the more time he spends on it, and it's awful hard to guess how long it would take. If he's a real perfectionist, he could spend a whole winter on it and enjoy it. Some people slap them together in no time and then they have leak problems for the rest of their lives." Later, he said in disbelief, "We found that some people were installing screws with a hammer instead of a screwdriver."

There is an apocryphal story that the Sunfish was designed so that Aileen, Alex Bryan's wife, would have a place to put her feet and sail comfortably after she became pregnant. Actually, Cort told me, the Sunfish was designed because both his wife and Aileen, who was Cornelius Shields' daughter, were uncomfortable sailing the Sailfish. "I didn't like it myself."

Nobody seems to remember whether the first Sunfish was built in 1952, '53 or '54. Cort does remember that the lines were lofted by the

15

Super Sailfish specifications:
Length .... 13 ft. 7 in.
Beam .... 35½ in.
Sail area .... 75 sq. ft.
Hull weight .... 98 lbs.

Sunfish specifications:
Length .... 13 ft. 10 in.
Beam .... 48½ in.
Sail area .... 75 sq. ft.
Hull weight .... 139 lbs.

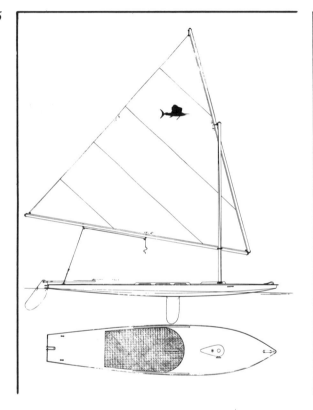

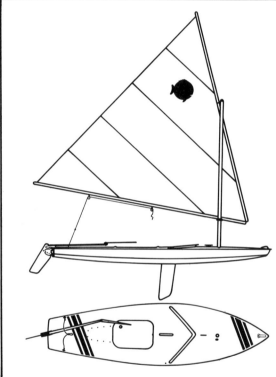

little company's first employee, Carl Meinert, right on the shop floor.

"They looked pretty good, and that was it," Cort said.

The boat's length was 13 feet 7½ inches, the beam ½ inch shy of 4 feet. The sail area, like that of the Super Sailfish, was 75 square feet. The hull weighed 130 pounds. The original Sunfish had a lot of parts in common with the Super Sailfish. The transom, rudder and spars were identical although the daggerboard was longer to compensate for the deeper hull.

The original Sunfish flyer lists the following specifications: "The best marine plywood and Philippine mahogany. Rudder, tiller, daggerboard, coamings, and rubbing strips are also mahogany. Mast and spars are selected Sitka spruce. Fittings are brass, bronze, and aluminum. Sail is specially treated mildew-resistant white sailcloth." In those days, sailcloth meant cotton. The picture shows a beautifully setting 10-panel cotton sail. It also shows a wraparound coaming like a horseshoe, starting where the present splashrail starts, and wrapping clean around the cockpit at the rails.

Heyniger designed the original flip-up rudder mechanism, which was made of bronze. Alcort switched to a different aluminum design a few years ago because the original fitting had a tendency to pop out when subjected to considerable side pressure in heavy air, causing you to lose control, an infuriating business. Many people modified their old Sunfish at considerable expense and effort to take the new, more satisfactory mount.

Heyniger also designed the gooseneck

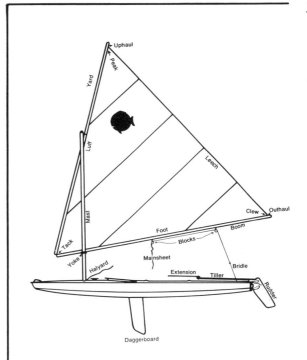

The front page of the second Sunfish brochure pictures Alex Bryan heading for the dock after a test sail. The first brochure was a simple one-page bulletin.

Let's Go Sailing

THE NEW Sunfish

WITH THE NEW ALCORT

Sunfish®

although he had help from Wilcox-Crittenden. "We didn't know about shrinkage of bronze," remembered Heyniger, "so the cast part was actually smaller than the pattern, but that was all right. It was already heavier than it needed to be. The casting shop, however, jumped with glee everytime we ordered another 100. You buy castings by the pound!"

Who designed the famous logo? "I guess I did," said Heyniger. "I took a nickel and drew a circle around it, drew a tail on, and a mouth and eye . . . and that's how it developed."

The original sails were white, but later the partners offered blue and red cotton.

Along about the time the first Sunfish was developed, Alcort acquired an advertising agency named Gotham. The account executive was Duncan Sutphen. He turned out the first few flyers and brochures. Shortly after that, Cort and Alex decided to look for an agency closer to Waterbury, and called the Graceman Agency in Hartford. My partner, John Brotherhood, was an account executive at the Graceman shop. One day, Ed Graceman called his staff together and asked, "Does anybody know anything about sailboats?" John was the only one who did, so he became Alcort's second advertising man.

"There were two nice guys sitting in the middle of a pile of shavings," John says of his first visit to Alcort. "I can remember two major marketing pronouncements I made to Bud (Cort) and Alex. The first was that they should establish a network of dealers, and stop trying to be just a mail-order operation. It took awhile, but they finally agreed, and I was right. The second pronouncement was that the Sunfish would never sell. I thought the Sailfish was unique, but that the Sunfish was trying too much to be a real boat. Oh well, .500 isn't too bad."

The Sailfish was phased out by 1962, but the Super Sailfish lived on for quite a while, in and out of production at some 100 to 200 boats per year. Now it too is no longer available.

The next big step that Cort and Alex took was to hire a young MBA from the University of Michigan, who wanted to be in the sailboat business. "He was the one that kind of drove us along," Cort says. "He was a big help to us." His name was Bruce Connolly, and the date was June, 1956.

In 1958, having outgrown the third plant they had taken over, Alcort designed and built its own plant. They were still building wooden boats. "Then, in 1959, Joe Schmidt of Naugatuck Chemical convinced us to try fiberglass," Bruce says. "Their technicians came in and taught us how to build with it. We started with the Super Sailfish, and built that for a year. In 1960 we started building the Sunfish in fiberglass.

"A number of changes were made for the shift to glass. The hull was made deeper, and the boat was given a little more freeboard forward to help reduce the original boat's tendency to submarine before the wind. The deck was given a little crown, and the chines were rounded to make them stronger and more easily removed from the molds. It was also an inch wider, because of the flanges where hull and deck were joined. It also became 2½ inches longer."

The glass and wood Super Sailfish, being almost identical in shape and weight, were competitive. But the fiberglass Sunfish was a faster boat in most conditions than the wooden one. I had a wooden Sunfish for a couple of years, and actually managed to win a regatta with it. It had absorbed a lot of water, and was much heavier than the average glass boat. This proved to be an advantage in light, puffy conditions, where the weight helped carry you through the lulls. Bob Bowles, the third World Champion, was another who started with a wood Sunfish—he built it himself—but after a year or so he also switched to glass.

The boats are built by the hand lay-up method, inside female molds. This is a quality way to build a boat, and is still used, even though newer chopper gun methods of building small boats have been developed.

First a layer of gelcoat is sprayed in. After the gelcoat comes a layer of resin. The fiberglass mat is squeegeed into it, and more resin is applied. A woven roving layer is next, giving the Sunfish its long-lasting strength, followed by more resin. The molds hang from the track from fore and aft bars, so that they can be flipped upside down and the raw hull, cockpit tub, or deck can be shaken out.

Styrofoam blocks are glued in with additional foam-in-place polystyrene and then the decks are glued on. Then comes a Rube Goldberg step. About a hundred heavy spring-loaded clamps are snapped into place around the circumference to bond the joint until it is dry. The workers who do that must be strong enough to pop tennis balls with their bare

*The gelcoat for the deck
stripes is applied between strips of
masking tape.*

hands! Before the deck is placed on the hull,
of course, the cockpit tub, daggerboard well and
mast well have been properly positioned.

After the hull/deck flange has been routed
to the proper dimension, the aluminum rub rail
is pop-riveted on, and the fittings are screwed
into oak blocks that have previously been glued
to the inside of the hull and deck. A hole is
drilled for the drainage plug, and then the hull is
tested for leaks. Pressure is applied through the
drain hole, and all seams are coated with soapy
water. But in spite of careful quality control,
leakers do occasionally show up.

For many years, the weights of the boats
varied considerably, depending on how careful
the workers were in applying the resin to the
fiberglass. I know from personal observation
that Alcort has tried to improve its quality control in this area, so that now most hulls are
closer to their advertised weight.

In molding the deck, a lot of masking tape
is used to put those bars sinister in place.
When did the deck striping come in? "That
was about '65 or '66," said Bruce. "They said
it could not be done, so I forget what show I
went to but I started striping the boats myself
with a shiny-faced tape. It was so successful
at the show that I was selling rolls of tape
for a short time, until Carl Meinert discovered
how to stripe the foredecks. That went along
for a couple of years until we needed something
new, and then we started to stripe the afterdeck as well. Now, they can't build a boat without striping because of the burning of the
molds."

With the introduction of fiberglass came

other new materials. The spars became aluminum, and the sails were offered in nylon and then in dacron. Alcort does not make fittings, or mold its own plastic or aluminum parts, but almost everything else is made at the Alcort plant in Waterbury, Connecticut. Since 1979, Sunfish have also been manufactured in Holland, under license to Ten Cate (pronounced Kata), a big Dutch conglomerate, and in Canada by Koma Boats of Clinton, Ontario. New plants will be started in 1983 in Chile and Uruguay. Sails for the European boat are also made by Fogh, in his Danish loft.

Looking back on the boat's development, Bruce Connolly says that a major innovation, from a marketing viewpoint, was "the discovery of the dePersia bailer. It went into both the wooden kit and the fiberglass boat. Up until then, you had to carry a bailing can. I remember having to tell people that and being very embarrassed in doing so."

A major change in the Sunfish design was the inclusion of a storage well molded as part of the cockpit tub, under the afterdeck. This is undoubtedly very handy for day sailing, and even for racing if you want to carry along a lunch or a bottle of water or stow your life jacket out of the way. But in heavy air, it becomes a big water trap, and was rather resented by the serious racers for a few years. Now, most of us are sailing newer Sunfish, so we all have the same handicap. Nevertheless, some people still inflate a beach ball inside the storage well to reduce its capacity for water. I once drew a design on paper for a drawer with a gasket around the forward edge to fit snugly

into the well. Alcort considered it for a while, but as far as I know they never went as far as to try out the design in practice. They now provide a nifty soft-side storage cooler as standard equipment.

Nobody seems to remember, anymore, just how much the first Sunfish cost. Neither Cort nor Alex kept many records during the early days. "We'd get so cluttered up with stuff that we'd throw a bunch away," they say. "And you forget to save one of everything." They think the first Sailfish cost $128.50 and that the first Sunfish was priced at $195, so that it was under the $200 mark.

I think they may be over-compensating for inflation. The first flyer, of which I think I possess the only surviving copy, boasts a price of $386 F.O.B. Waterbury. And I have another flyer, dated 1963, that lists the Sunfish kit at $297, and the fiberglass Sunfish at $476. In the same flyer, the standard Sailfish kit is $209, the Super Sailfish kit $239, and the fiberglass Super Sailfish $394.

At one time, the price of Alcort's boats was rigidly maintained by the dealers. Then, for a while, thanks to the Robinson Patman Act and similar laws, retail prices were not even suggested. Even without controlling pricing, however, Sunfish now cost almost triple what they did when I first started sailing them. Nevertheless, a Sunfish is probably one of the best-built toys around. A few years ago, *Fortune* named it one of the best American-made products. I have owned more of them than I can remember, and I never sold one for less than I paid for it.

The Alcort story is an exception to the old rule that nice guys finish last. As Bruce Connolly says of Alex and Cort, "They were great people to work for, absolutely the best. They were like a father image to me. Alex and Cort were literally two of the nicest guys I've ever known."

By the mid-60s, the business was growing ever-larger and the partners decided it was time to sell. "We were growing so rapidly that we felt we either had to go public, which we didn't particularly want to do, or find a larger financial partner. We picked AMF for a certain amount of synergism with the other AMF sports and leisure products. We needed greater financial backing."

In 1969, the partners sold Alcort to AMF. They believe the decision was a good one. The Sunfish, which had always been their mainstay, continued in production and, by 1982, over 200,000 had been built and sold.

● **Class Development**

The early Sunfish racing was all doubles. Bruce Connolly wanted to promote the Sunfish as a family boat, and most of the early sailors seemed to like it that way. However, the serious sailors agitated for single-handed racing, and in 1966 Sunfish singles were added at the National Championships. Even in that first year, the singles fleet was approximately three times the size of the doubles fleet. After a couple of years, Alcort decided to hold Singles and Doubles Championships at the same time in two different places. That preserved doubles racing for a year or two more, but now about the only

doubles race left is the Great Long-Distance Down-the-Connecticut-River Race.

The Sunfish introduced sailing to a whole new group of people—younger people mostly, who could not afford the bigger boats of the time or membership in a yacht club. For the Sunfish you didn't need a club, or a mooring, or a boatyard, or all the other expenses associated with those upper class symbols. You carried the boat on top of your car, launched it from a beach, and never needed a boatyard because the boat never needed maintenance. Those were the qualities that made the Sunfish the largest fiberglass one-design class in the world.

What made it the largest fiberglass one-design *racing* class in the world was the fierceness with which its one-design nature was protected. In the first place, it was the first manufacturer-owned class to achieve popularity. The class organization is a dictatorship, not a democracy. But it is a benevolent dictatorship, and while there have been a few attempts to take over the class on a more democratic basis, most Sunfish sailors would just as soon leave things to Alcort. Their wishes are well represented by an advisory committee, which is usually consulted before any major changes are made.

Bruce Connolly feels that the most important contribution the Sunfish has made to yacht racing is the concept of manufacturer control. Only in that way, he feels, has the unique one-design nature of the boat been maintained. He points to the Laser and the J/24 as proof. It's a point well taken, I think. Those sailors who have been dissatisfied with Alcort control want the class to allow sailors more leeway,

One of the first fiberglass Super Sail-fish, with first sales manager Bruce Connolly aboard. Bruce is credited by most Sunfish old-timers with building the class to its present pre-eminence.

23

including opening up the sails to all sail makers. I am glad Alcort has resisted.

What changes and additions have been permitted over the years—and the class rules now permit 22—have been permitted primarily to improve convenience and safety. It is still quite possible to take a boat right out of the box and win races against boats that have been completely equipped with all of the gadgetry permitted.

Because the Sunfish is controlled completely by the manufacturer, it has remained as one-design a boat as is possible. Well, almost. Both before and since the company's purchase by AMF, Alcort has resisted the temptation to play the planned obsolescence game. It has made some changes over the years, a couple of which have been allowed to make the boat a little faster, but they were made primarily for competitive market reasons, usually with the concurrence of the racing class.

The Sail

The first major change, made towards the end of 1967, was a better-cut sail. The sail of the very first Sailfish was made by Ratsey and Lapthorn, although Alcort bought them from Old Town—the canoe company—for a couple of years before they discovered they could buy them directly from Ratsey. Every Sailfish, Super Sailfish, and Sunfish sail until 1979 was made by Ratsey. The original sails were cut very flat, and lacked power under many conditions. So, in 1967, the decision was made to change the pattern, and produce a fuller sail. Alcort made one of the few tactical errors in its marketing history when it tried to keep the change secret. Sailors soon discovered that the new sail was faster, however, and within a year or year-and-a-half, anyone with serious competitive ambitions had to switch to the new sail. For a while, there was a certain mystique about those Ratsey sails, and suspicion of Alcort. In certain fleets, sailors became convinced that only sails with a serial number ending in M on the Ratsey label were really competitive, but that conviction did not prove out in major competition.

Bruce Connolly recently told me the reason for that change. The Sunfish had spawned a number of competitors, and finally one of them, the Scorpion, came through with a sail with a little bit more draft. "It took a fleet away—it knocked our fleet out in one of the lakes in Mississippi, a very fine Sunfish fleet in Mississippi. We just took care of that by having Ratsey make a decent dacron sail and shipped it down to the dealer, who happened to be the best sailor in the fleet. Literally, once he put this thing on the water, that was the end of the Scorpion." The 1967 sail was a copy of that winner, and the pattern for all sails until 1978.

In 1978 and 1979, Hans Fogh of Canada, a transplanted Dane who had learned his sailing and sailmaking from the greatest one-design sailor of all time, four-time Olympic champion Paul Elvström, was asked by Alcort to design the ultimate Sunfish sail. After much testing, the design was fixed, and manufacture of Sunfish sails was transferred to Fogh's plant in Canada.

The only other exception to Ratsey's unbroken monopoly on Sunfish sailmaking was during the late '60s and early '70s, when Sunfish were manufactured in Canada, and Fogh produced some sails to the Ratsey design. These were sold only in Canada, except for a final batch of 50 that were left over when manufacture in Canada ended. The 50 were sold to summer camps and resorts, so that the chance they would be used for anything but intramural competition would be very slim. As far as I know, none ever showed up at a major regatta. They were beautifully made sails, with leather patches at the corners, and stronger grommets on the foot and luff. The current Fogh sails are also better made than the Ratsey sails.

There was an interesting phenomenon both times new sails were introduced. Even though the new sails were in time proved to be faster than the old, it took a while for the top sailors to get used to the differences. Even though the new sails had been in use all summer in 1968, I managed to win the North Americans with the old-style sail, primarily, I think, because I was used to it. Early in 1969, it became apparent that I was outclassed with the old sail, and I switched to the new one.

A similar phenomenon occurred in 1979, the first full season with the new Fogh sail. Alan Beckwith won the North Americans with his old, well-blown-out Ratsey sail, as did Joe Blouin in 1980. But at the 1981 North Americans, Paul Odegard won with a Fogh sail, having reluctantly abandoned his old favorite Ratsey early in the season. Mike Catalano, who is still at this writing convinced that the Fogh

So popular is the Sunfish in resort areas that one of them, the Bahamas, immortalized the craft on a postage stamp.

sail was no improvement on his Ratsey, wound up a dismal—for him—sixth.

At this writing, it appears that the Ratsey sail is still competitive in relatively light air and flat water, but that the more powerful Fogh sail is faster in wind and waves. Here's what Olympic silver medalist Hans Fogh had to say about the sails in *Windward Leg*, the company's newsletter, in 1980:

"Sunfish sailing is not new to me . . . I sailed in my first Sunfish Worlds in 1972 in Bermuda. I have always felt that the Sunfish sail was too flat and I know that many sailors go to great lengths to stretch their sails until they attain a fast shape.

"After developing the sail design for the Apollo sailboat, I discussed my ideas for an improved Sunfish sail with Eric Skemp, then V. P. Marketing at AMF Alcort. At first he was hesitant because of the strict class rules, but after sailing in the 10th Worlds in the Netherlands, he too became aware of the dissatisfaction with the old design.

"We decided to experiment with new designs to see if we could come up with a faster sail. Our goal was to produce a sail that would be competitive when new, as opposed to the old design that required careful and time-consuming stretching. Our intention was to help the new sailor be instantly competitive . . . or at least have an equal chance. . . .

"Thinking about the sail, I decided that it would have to fit all weight ranges and give no advantage to any one group. For example, too full a sail would help the heavy person in heavy air whereas a flat sail would give advantage to

the light person. During our testing, I discovered that by moving the boom on the gooseneck, or by changing the position of the halyard on the gaff, one could change the helm or cause the gaff to bend, both of which help to adapt the boat to different sizes of people. Therefore, with these adjustments in mind, I decided that a medium shape was necessary.

"During the fall I tried many sail shapes and different types of cloth. I would have preferred to change to 3.8-ounce cloth, but that would have doubled the cost of the sail. I decided to continue using the 3-ounce Fleetboat cloth, which has proven itself acceptable in the 30-year history of the class.

"To remove many of the wrinkles from the sail, I rotated the top and bottom panels so that the thread direction lined up with the stretch. These sails looked good and performed very well when tested against other Sunfish on Lake Ontario.

"These sails were given their final stamp of approval by Alcort and the class at the 11th Sunfish World Championship in Aruba. Even in the very heavy air of Aruba (20-35 knots), most sailors found ways to adjust the sail for comfort and speed. I found that with the Hookanson rig, these sails were very good in heavy air and their performance in light and medium air has since been shown to be excellent.

"What exactly had I done to the sail design? Firstly, I put a lot of broad seaming into the sail. Next, I cut the luff of the sail to match the bending characteristics of the luff boom. Then I matched the foot curve to that of the boom. To ensure there was no fluttering on the leech, I hollowed it. To each corner, I added dacron reinforcing for durability. For strength, the luff and foot tape was beefed up and all 28 grommets used were spur grommets, which have teeth to grab into the cloth.

"To be sure that every sail is absolutely the same—to maintain the one-design concept—the cloth used has a style number to ensure that it is woven to the same specifications. A testing program has been set up for the cloth with a tolerance of no more or less than two percent, as well. In addition, we have made up exact mylar patterns for everything, from the panels to the reinforcing, in order to have uniformity from the first sail to the millionth."

● **The Daggerboard**

The other big Sunfish changes have been in daggerboard design. The first change, in the early '70s, replaced the original round-bottom board with what Alcort called the "Shadow Shape" board. It was a disaster, because it had less surface area than the old. Every serious competitor soon found he had to have an old board if he wanted to have a chance at winning. In the World Championships, competitors were all issued the new boards, so everything was supposed to be even. But a number of the Americans felt they were handicapped, because they were used to the old board. The Caribbean sailors, however, were accustomed to competing against each other year-round with the new board, since they adopted Sunfishing after the new board came in. As a matter of fact, in 1973 and 1974, Caribbean sailors won the Worlds.

What was the reason for the change? "Don't blame me; blame yourselves," Bruce told me. "You're the guys who made so much of a fuss about the shape of the board. The whole racing class kept saying it wasn't right, it didn't do this, it didn't do that. Don't forget that it was about the time the Laser was coming along and the Laser had the shaved board. So I went to Fred Scott (the Alcort designer at the time and responsible for the Force 5) and said, 'Okay, go ahead and do it equal to or better.' So he came up with a thing that was equal to or better. I didn't know anything about airfoil sections and all that, so he gave them a shape that looked more modern."

Finally, in 1980, AMF Alcort came out with a third board, after testing it among several top sailors during the 1979-80 frostbite season of the Barrington, Rhode Island, fleet. The Barrington board, as it became known, has the same area as the very first board, but also has an angled bottom tip like the newer "Shadow Shape" design. It seems to be as fast as the old board, but many sailors are, at this writing, still convinced that the original board is best.

Alcort has made a number of other changes over the years, some of which made the racing sailors nervous, but in time the new boats were shown to be just as fast as the old one. Some of the earliest changes were made before serious competition started in the class—the switch from wood to fiberglass; the switch from cotton to nylon and then finally to dacron. To be competitive, you had to have a fiberglass boat with dacron sail. I never came across a wooden mast in competition, although the original Sunfish masts were wood.

Mast and Rigging

The first significant change made in the racing model—at least the first one of which I was aware—was a switch from a tapered aluminum mast to a straight round section. For a very short time, some sailors were convinced that the tapered mast had to be faster, because it had to be lighter at the head. However, in spite of the logic of this position, it became evident that there was no difference. We balanced the masts on a fulcrum to see if the head was, indeed, lighter, and proved to ourselves that it wasn't. We then learned that the masts were tapered by thickening the wall section, which explained the apparent anomaly.

Eyebolt

A year or two after that, Alcort switched from using an eyebolt and pulley at the head of the mast to the simple plastic fitting with a hole in it used today. This change caused some consternation with at least one of the top competitors, who felt that the inherent looseness of the block system allowed the rig to "breathe." We pointed out to him that the rig could "breathe" just as well if he left an inch or two of slack in the halyard. At the same time, Alcort switched to one-piece plastic caps at the ends of the spars, eliminating the need for an eyebolt. Since this lightened up the rig a trifle, no one objected. There was some worry that the flimsy looking plastic would break easily, but that has produced fewer problems than the old eyebolts, which used to come loose from their

Three daggerboards are permissible on a Sunfish but all must have been made by Alcort. Illustrated (left to right) *are all three: old style, new style and Barrington.*

27

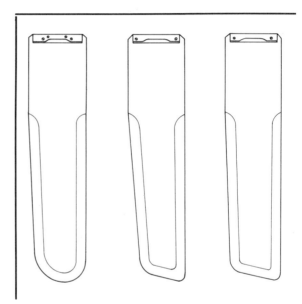

The foredeck of earlier Sunfish models was subject to scratching by a bolt projecting through the boom. A sail clip pop-riveted to the boom, or a sleeve slid over the boom, affords protection.

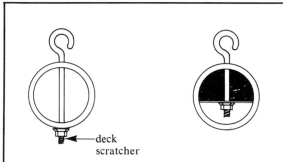

1. *Early model boom.*   2. *This won't scratch . . .*

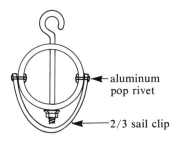

3. *. . . neither will this.*

nuts because of road vibration when traveling.

Those pesky eyebolts are still used at the forward end of the spars, to hook them together. Because the eyebolt and the boom thrust down towards the deck, more than one Sunfish has had a half-moon scratch dug into its foredeck, when the sail dropped low because of a loose halyard. Alcort has wrestled with a better system, and has produced a plastic acorn nut that has reduced the problem. For older boats, the best protection I have heard proposed is as follows. You take off the cap on the forward end of the boom, slip in the bearing block, drill through it from the top, insert the shorter eyebolt, put a lock nut and washer inside the boom against the bearing block, tighten it up, and replace the cap. Then, if the boom drags across the deck, the smooth plastic end fitting will rub, not the sharp bolt end. Like some other fixes on the Sunfish, this one would probably not be questioned by an inspection committee. Another way to protect the deck from the eyebolt is to slip two-thirds of a sailset around the boom over the nut, fastened with machine screws or pop rivets, to act as a skid.

All these changes bring the Sunfish class up to date as of 1982. Additional material about how to set up each of the boat's hull and rig components will be found in later chapters.

● **Super Sunfish**

The Super Sunfish grew out of an idea first proposed in the early '60s by one of the real Sunfish class stalwarts, John Black Lee of New Canaan, Connecticut. Like many other sailors, he was bothered by the aerodynamic inefficiency of the lateen rig, and started playing around with ways to put a more conventional high aspect ratio rig on the Sunfish hull. He experimented with spars and sails from other one-design classes, and tried to get Alcort interested in the idea. Alcort, with what was probably good marketing judgment, decided not to mess around with a good thing.

In 1972, John decided to launch a more sophisticated version of the Sunfish on his own. With Alcort's help, he put together a high-performance rig using a single-piece, tapered spar, midboom sheeting and **a** traveler inside the forward edge of the cockpit.

The point of all the added controls is to enable a racer to change the aerodynamics of the sail. With various combinations of the line tension, the draft can be moved forward or aft, the leech may be tightened or loosened, the chord—the sail's depth in cross-section—flattened or deepened. The midboom sheeting permits the sail shape to be retained while changing the sail's angle to the center line of the boat, easing out in the puffs and trimming in as the boat picks up speed.

John christened his new Sunfish version the Formula S. In two or three years, more than 200 were being raced and there was a North American championship and a Grand Prix circuit. Things were going swimmingly and the boat was chosen for the Interclass Solo Championship, sailed singlehanded each year in three different classes.

By the time the Formula S had established itself, Alcort—now AMF—tacitly acknowledged

30 the error of its original decision to produce a more sophisticated Sunfish. Under the guidance of Jack Evans, the company began development of its own high-performance rig. The new version was introduced at the New York Boat Show in 1974 and was labelled the Super Sunfish.

Since then, the class has grown slowly and activity has been primarily in the Northeast. There, it is quite strong, with many of the top Sunfish sailors jumping into Super Sunfish for the major regattas. Two or three regattas feature weekend racing, with the Sunfish on one day and the Super on the other. In addition, there is a year-end Light Corinthian combination Sunfish/ Super Sunfish regatta to cap off the season and the North Americans.

The Super Sunfish concept seems to be a good one. It gives the racer a chance to sail the Sunfish for pure tiller-wiggling competition and then to jump into the Super to add the new dimension of aerodynamic sail control, even while hiked out in a stiff breeze, thanks to the double leads on most of its control lines. The Super Sunfish is a lot different boat than the basic Sunfish. It feels different and requires different sailing techniques. It's not better than a Sunfish; it's just different. To my mind, it is like owning two boats for less than the price of a boat and a half. For sailors who have ambitions of moving up into higher performance sailing, such as the Olympic classes, a Super rig will provide a lot of teaching before one invests in a more delicate, expensive machine.

2 *Ashore and Afloat*

32 Nine out of 10 Sunfish owners do not race. They just sail casually and have a lot of fun. But, whether you intend to race or not, you should master the basics of launching, sailing, and, in general, handling the boat. That is what this chapter is all about.

● Transportation

There are many ways to transport a Sunfish. The boats are comparatively easy to move about and people who don't have to travel far to the water often slip a Sunfish into the back of a station wagon. Perhaps the most popular method of carrying the boat, however, is on top of a car.

Most any kind of luggage rack will do, although wooden bars shaped to the crown of the deck and padded with carpet provide the best protection. In an emergency, a couple of old tires wrapped in some kind of cloth provide just enough stability and protection for both car and boat, assuming the boat is well tied down. That's a very important point no matter how you transport your Sunfish. I know of at least a dozen boats that have required extensive repairs after flying off alone down the highway. It is a testimonial to the boat's ruggedness that I've never heard of one being completely demolished in this way. But it's not something you want to do just for the fun of spending your money.

I once made a rack of galvanized water pipe to fit on a convertible. It looked rather like a giant iron bedstead, but it served its purpose well. It fit over the car top, the legs supported on the four fenders. Each leg ended in a large suction cup. It was even possible to raise and lower the top with a Sunfish in place on the carrier. I fastened the boat down with specially adjustable lines, each with a hook to grab the bumper, a tent line toggle to snug the line down, and a spring to absorb road shocks. I had this rig for quite a while and used it on three different convertibles. Finally, I got tired of lifting the boat on and off the carrier and bought a trailer.

Trailers are certainly convenient ways of getting your Sunfish to the water and almost any sort of trailer will do. Most people have trailers that carry their boats right side up, but some carry them upside down so that the bottom doesn't get gunked up with road tar and scratches. A full boat cover can be used to protect the entire hull from road dirt.

The Sunfish is a rugged boat but it should be well supported on its trailer. If you let the hull rest on supports between the chine and keel, especially under the cockpit tub, flexing will occur and this will eventually cause cracks. I had one Sunfish that eventually split right along the chine. (I did learn, however, that this boat had been made by a Texas firm under subcontract to Alcort and that it and others suffered from a lack of adequate resin. At that time, in the early '60s, Alcort had outrun its own production capacity.)

I have seen as many as four Sunfish carried on the standard Sunfish-style trailer, and even more on special heavy-duty rigs. Racer Tom Ehman had the misfortune to flip a four-boat rig on his way to the North Americans in the mid-70s. The center of gravity was too high.

Sunfish can be carried on a roof rack, on specially made pipe racks if you own a convertible, or even nestled in the back of a station wagon.

Alcort does supply extra bunks to make a two-boat rig out of the standard trailer. This works very well. Some owners build racks that sit between two Sunfish and put all the weight on the bottom boat. Most Sunfish thus burdened seem to survive. I used to carry two boats on an Alligator trailer but eventually broke both springs. I had a truck-spring-repair garage install new heavy-duty springs and haven't had problems since.

The biggest problem I have found with trailers is that the electrical systems go bad very easily. It is important to make sure that the wiring is fastened to the frame at many points. Otherwise, the constant flexing will work-harden the wire and eventually break it. Fittings of all kinds seem to rust easily on lights and connectors. I finally made a lighting rig that attaches to the rudder fitting of the boat itself. This rides nice and high and is easily seen by following motorists. When the trip is complete, I can stow the lights in the trunk of the car, protected from the elements. I have found that, even though I usually keep a cover over boat and trailer, the lighting system still seems to deteriorate. It is a problem you have to keep up with.

How best to carry spars? A couple of companies make spar carriers. These are usually two-piece affairs, one attaching to the rudder fitting, the other sitting in the mast hole. They seem to work very well. I carry my spars on H-shaped wooden bunks that are well-padded with carpeting. One sits over the mast hole, the other just behind the cockpit. I secure the spars with shock cord. Larry Lewis used to do

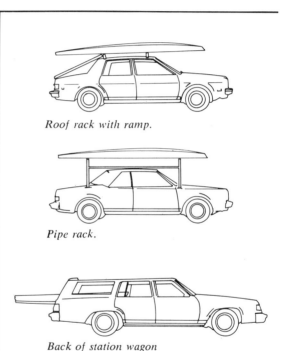

Roof rack with ramp.

Pipe rack.

Back of station wagon

just fine with a couple of old 12-inch tires, resting the spars atop them.

● **From Shore to Water**

Having arrived at the beach, how do you get the boat from car to water? At most regattas, there are plenty of people around, and most boats are simply carried down to the water. But a number of commercial dollies are available, and many sailors have fashioned their own. These seem to fall into three categories.

First, there is the miniature trailer, which is a set of wheels with a long handle and bunks to drop the boat on. These are easy to use but are difficult to transport. Second, and for many years the most popular, is a rig that slips up into the daggerboard well, leaving two wheels under the hull to roll on. Third, there are dollies that attach to the transom, either clipping to the bridle eyes or the rudder mount.

All these methods are better than dragging the boat over a rocky beach. Whatever kind of dolly you use, you will want relatively large wheels, both in diameter and tread width. Otherwise, the dolly will be hard to hustle through sand. One of the neatest rigs I've seen was homemade. It attached to the transom and used an inflatable yacht bumper as a roller —the kind with the hole through the middle. A piece of pipe was slipped through the hole as an axle. Another rig used what looked like a light plane tire inner tube, barely inflated, to support the boat and glide over the sand. I once made a dolly out of bicycle wheels. They made up in diameter what they lacked in tread width. The sheer size of the thing, however,

made me abandon it.

One commercially made gadget that didn't last long on the market combined a roof rack and dolly. The problem was that the wheels were too small. You had to trundle the Sunfish along sideways, which meant you needed a wide swath of beach all to yourself. When you got to the car, you hooked the handles of this wheelbarrow-like contraption to the racks on top of the roof, walked around and lifted. The whole rig telescoped into the roof racks and, if you were patient and didn't rush things so the mechanism jammed, you were ready to go. I've also seen some homemade rigs that provided ramps up the trunk of the car to the roof.

The most difficult transfer I can remember involved a rented pick-up truck camper in which we attended the North Americans at Gananoque, Quebec. I carried the boat on top of the camper. Getting the boat there was no problem because my driveway had high banks on either side. But when we reached the yacht club at Gananoque, it took a crew of about six friends on the ground and two or three atop the camper to get the boat down, and even then we almost dropped it. As it happened, another contestant had a pick-up truck camper, too, but he planned ahead. He had a most ingenious derrick welded up of pipe. With it, he could load and unload by himself, with his wife just lending a hand —just like a yacht taking aboard its tender.

Chris Urfer had the simplest solution. Chris is not that big, but what there is of him is all muscle. He simply flipped his boat up over his head and portaged it, his head in the cock-

A Sunfish can be moved to the water with the aid of wheels that mount on either the rudder fitting or in the daggerboard slot.

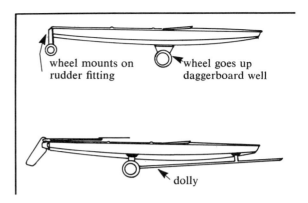

wheel mounts on rudder fitting

wheel goes up daggerboard well

dolly

pit—a strange shell-bearing sea creature. When he got to the car, he pressed the Sunfish over his head and slid it onto the racks. At the first Worlds, Jeorge Bruder of Brazil carried his boat to the water, fully rigged. Later, after a full day of racing, he carried it back up the beach. But he was a legend even in the Finn class, which abounds with muscular gorillas!

Launching from the Beach

Most Sunfish are sailed off the beach. This presents three possible scenarios: the wind may be blowing across the beach; it may be blowing onto the beach; it may be blowing off the beach. No matter which direction the wind blows from, there are a number of things to do before you think of actually pushing off into the water.

Get organized. Be sure the tiller is under the bridle, that the halyard is coiled out of the way, and that the end of the mainsheet is knotted—so that the sheet cannot run out of the block—and reachable from the cockpit. The daggerboard should be in the cockpit, with the top propped on the foredeck, so that it can be slipped easily into the slot once the boat is launched. The rudder, too, must be in the up position, for reasons that will soon be apparent.

If the wind is blowing up or down the beach, you can raise the sail with the boat heading straight down into the water. The sail will swing out to one side or the other, "weather-vaning" to the wind. It is best, however, always to point the bow into the wind before raising sail. Otherwise, if the sail fills before the boom lifts off the deck, the boom will swing around

and the tack bolt may gouge a curved track in the foredeck.

When launching, especially into a swell, the board and rudder are especially vulnerable. The swell can lift the hull clear of the bottom, letting the board or rudder drop down. Then the swell races back out and the boat drops down onto the bottom. If the boat has heeled at all, the board and rudder will hit with a sideways impact. The Sunfish's weight alone can now break them. If you have already jumped aboard, the daggerboard and rudder will sure-ly break.

The second type of launch, when the wind is blowing onto the beach, is more difficult than when the wind is blowing parallel to the shoreline, especially if the wind is strong.

The reason for this is that you will have the daggerboard down. You will be beating to windward off the shore, and that means you have to have the board down to prevent side-slip. If there are swells, you had better plan to wade out from shore, because the boat will slip back toward shore as you jump aboard, and you have to allow room to get that board down and time to get it biting into the water.

In such conditions, wade out up to your arm-pits, keeping the boat headed into the wind. Drop in the daggerboard, twist the boat so that you can climb in from the windward side—that is, push the bow away from you—and make sure the sheet is loose, so the boat won't try to sail away from you. Jump aboard, drop the rudder in quickly, pull in the sheet, and sail off. Make sure the sheet is free before you ever leave the beach! Once aboard, remain on the windward rail, or you may find yourself flat on your back in shallow water with the boat on top of you, a very uncomfortable position and one that can damage you or the spars when the next wave hits.

Obviously, it is best to get used to into-the-wind beach launching in light air, before you tackle big waves and stronger breezes.

The third launching condition is having the wind at your back as you face the water. If you try to raise the sail with the bow pointed towards the water, it will "weather-vane" a full 180 degrees, streaming out ahead of the boat. If your mainsheet has been reeved through a block on deck, the stopper knot in the sheet's end will stop the sail's outward swing and the boat can—if the wind is strong enough—be spun completely around.

There are two good methods for launching when the wind is off the beach. One is to launch the boat before hoisting sail, swing the bow into the wind, raise the sail and then jump aboard. You can take your time about lowering the rudder and slipping in the daggerboard since the wind will be pushing you offshore. The problem with this approach is that you have little or no steerageway. The boat may swing around so that the sail will fill as you hoist it. Once again, the danger arises of gouging the deck with the bolt at the tack where the boom joins the gaff.

The second way to launch with the wind is to point the bow up the beach and raise the sail. You can then launch the boat backwards into the water, jump aboard while the sail is still luffing, drop the rudder *before* you try to put in the board, then let the boat swing around until the sail fills. In this situation, you don't need to lower the board until the boat is sailing, since leeway is not a worry when you are sailing downwind.

It is quite possible, by the way, to sail a Sunfish backwards, a useful maneuver at times. Sometimes, people do it just for fun. The trick is to let the boat get some sternway with the sail luffing just enough so that the rudder will bite in. Steering a boat backwards is just like riding a coaster wagon. You turn the tiller so that the rudder end is pointing in the direction you want to go. Once you have learned to steer this way, with the sail luffing, you can then push the sail out to catch some wind on the "wrong" side, and away you go.

● **Launching from a Dock**

The principles involved in launching from a dock are similar to those in launching from a beach. Whenever possible, you want to be able to point the bow into the wind when you raise the sail. If you are on the windward side of a dock, and the dock is too high for the sail to swing out over it, you have a problem. The sail will fill before the boat has a chance to get some headway, and you will be plastered up against the dock. Any sharp projections on the dock will probably rip the sail.

Fortunately, it is not very difficult to paddle a Sunfish. Just paddle out away from the dock far enough to permit you to raise the sail, drop the rudder and daggerboard, and sail away before you drift back into the dock. Allow plenty of drifting room.

A rather awkward way to sail
a Sunfish. If both sailors would
slide their bottoms out over the
water they would be more comfortable and the boat would flatten
out, relieving the heavy weather
helm (note angle of rudder). It
would also help to slip the sheet
under the deck hook, which would
flatten the sail. Steering by foot is
one way to free up a hand, but it's
not comfortable for long.

If you must raise the sail from the windward side of a dock, you may be able to do so with the help of a second person. Lift the boom up and hand it to your friend on the dock, and have him hold it so that the boom is pointing dead into the wind. Raise the sail *quickly* and hope that the wind does not shift too much for your friend to keep up with. If he stands right on the edge of the dock, of course, your boat itself can be pointing right into the wind, since the boom extends over the transom. If the wind does shift before he can shove you off, you will "weather-vane" around and be plastered helplessly against the dock. Before raising sail, have the rudder and dagger-board down. Then, when your friend gives a good shove from the end of the boom, you will shoot out with some steerageway and be able to bear off and sail away. Leaving a dock like this, however, is a tricky maneuver, at best.

● **How to Sit in a Sunfish**

Obviously, if you are just sailing for fun, you will sit any way that feels comfortable. You should know, however, the most efficient way to sit in the boat, just in case you want to get someplace fast someday. The Sunfish wants to sail flat on the water under most conditions. That means fore-and-aft as well as side-to-side.

Under most conditions, you should sit with your weight at the forward edge of the cockpit. The neophyte sailor wants to face forward, with the tiller right alongside his hip. This yields poor control and makes the stern drag in the water. Sit sideways on the windward side of the boat. It may feel awkward at first, but it gives you full control of the boat. Your aft hand controls the tiller—get used to using the tiller extension instead of the tiller itself—and your forward hand controls the mainsheet. Sitting sideways, you can control the side-to-side trim of the boat easily by moving in and out.

Because the wind is often puffy, you will be moving in and out fairly often, and you will want to be able to slide. That is why few serious Sunfish sailors put antislip strips on the deck. You may, however, want them in the bottom of the cockpit.

On a warm, lazy day, you may want to drop into the cockpit, sitting forward in the well with your legs curled up beside you. It may sound uncomfortable, but it soon becomes second nature. Or you can just flop down into the cockpit in a sitting position, with your legs spread out on the foredeck and your back leaning against the after edge of the cockpit. That's when a urethane life jacket becomes not only a safety feature but a cushion as well. Use it as a backrest. Just remember that a sudden puff can conceivably dump you before you can climb out.

● **Safety on the Water**

Unless I am sailing on a very small lake in mild weather, I almost always wear a racing life vest. I am, perhaps, overcautious, but I have seen summer squalls come out of nowhere on the nicest of days, capsizing whole fleets of sailboats. Usually, there is some warning, but some squalls come in from a totally unexpected direction, catch the sail aback, and flip a boat over

before the sailor knows what's happening. In one instance I know of, the boom cracked the sailor's head, knocking him overboard and stunning him long enough so that he became separated from the boat, which drifted off. Fortunately, he was wearing a life jacket. There was another boat nearby and he was rescued.

Even if you don't wear a life jacket, at least have one aboard. The Coast Guard requires one for each person aboard.

Whether or not you're wearing a life jacket, remember that a Sunfish will not sink, even if it is punctured and filled with water. The boat is equipped with foam flotation and, as long as you stay with your Sunfish, you are all right. If the boat turns turtle and remains that way, with the mast pointing downwards, you may have trouble getting aboard, especially if the daggerboard has slipped out. (For this reason, Alcort recommends tying the board to the deck. The company now supplies the boat with a padeye on deck and hole in the daggerboard handle for just this purpose. A length of line is even included.) If the daggerboard floats away from you, a Sunfish is practically impossible to right. However, if the board falls out of the slot and you have it attached to the boat, you can swim beneath the hull, shove the board in, and prepare to right the boat.

Almost everyone who has sailed a Sunfish for any length of time has capsized it. Compared to a Finn or a Laser, the Sunfish is a very stable boat, but stable is a relative term. When you are racing hard, trying to get the most out of the boat in a stiff breeze, you will eventually find yourself in the water. For this reason, it is a good idea to practice capsizing on purpose.

If you capsize to leeward and your reflexes are fast enough, it is quite possible to lean forward over the windward side of the boat, swing your legs up and over, and land on the daggerboard just as the sail hits the water. While on the board, hold on to the windward edge of the hull, lean your tail out over the water, and the boat will pop right back up. Again, if your reflexes are fast enough, you can pull yourself back into the boat with that same pivot-on-your-stomach movement, and never get anything but your socks wet. I used to do this before the start of every light-air race, having convinced myself that a wet sail was faster than a dry one.

Should you find yourself in the water alongside your Sunfish, shake the water out of your eyes, make sure the daggerboard is in the trunk all the way, and swim around the boat until you're at the place where the board emerges. Do not let the boat get away from you. Now reach up and pull yourself onto the daggerboard. This may be enough to right the boat. If it isn't, because you are too light, stand up on the board and back out to its very end, holding on to the side of the hull. You may have to lean out rather far in order to get this started, especially if the sail has filled with water. Watch the sail carefully. When it starts to lift, time things so that you can dive into the boat quickly, because it will suddenly jerk upright as it shakes the water loose from the sail.

If the boat doesn't want to right, it is probably because the sheet is still cleated in a close-hauled position. Just reach over into the cockpit

Sunfish can carry a surprising number of people, although four heavies like these shouldn't venture out in open water. This was part of a relay race at the sixth Worlds; another sailor was added at each leg of the race. (Bow to stern: the legendary Arthur Knapp, who raced America's J-boats in the '30s, and Sunfishers Bob Knapp—no relation—Henry De Wolfe, and former World Champion Bob Bowles.)

and free it. This should bring the boat upright, even if you weigh only 85 pounds.

Sometimes, especially if you fall to leeward into the cockpit as the boat capsizes, it will keep right on going and turn completely upside down, turn "turtle." When this happens, you should probably get to windward of the boat and, using the daggerboard, pull yourself onto the bottom. Make sure the board remains fully lowered. Then slip your feet over the side until your toes are on the narrow aluminum rub rail. Holding on to the tip of the daggerboard, lean backwards as far out as you can. The boat should slowly come up. If it does not, the spar is probably stuck in the mud.

In this case, you will have to go around to the other side of the boat—the lee side—and hope that the wind will help you slip the mast out of the mud as the boat comes up. If you try to right an inverted boat from the leeward side, the wind will catch under the sail as it comes up from the water, and probably capsize the boat back on top of you again, especially if you try to pull yourself in before the boat has steadied. For this reason, you should try to right the boat from the windward side if you possibly can. Then, when the sail comes up, you will be on the weather side, balancing the pressure on the sail. Once the boat has settled down, you should be able to pull yourself into the cockpit.

Capsizing can be frightening when it first happens. For this reason, it really makes sense to practice on a nice, calm, sunny day. Do it a few times until you have the feel of it. Then, if you capsize on a day when the wind is blow-

A relatively small sailor demonstrating beautiful heavy-air form. His feet are hooked about at the midpoint of the forward and aft lips of the cockpit, putting his center of gravity, about at his waist, well out over the water.

42

ing and the waves are trying to wash your breath away, you'll have some confidence in what you are doing. Like anything else, once you know how, righting a capsized Sunfish is easy.

Once you have righted the boat in a heavy wind, it is probably a good idea to let the sail luff a bit to shake off some water and let you get your breath back. The sudden exertion of the capsize and righting, especially if the water is cold, can take a lot out of you. When you have your breath back, sail off.

● **Staying Upright in Heavy Wind**

Even in 50 or 60 knots of wind, it is possible to sail on a reach in a Sunfish. You want to keep only the aft corner of sail drawing. You'll have to hike hard and may not be able to go in the direction you want, but you can get the feel of the boat.

If you want to go downwind in really heavy air, consider dropping the sail and sailing on under bare pole. You will find that you have plenty of steerageway.

It may be difficult or impossible to progress to windward in strong breezes. Just by reaching back and forth, however, you can stay off a lee shore. If all else fails, and you are worn out, drop the sail, roll it up and wrap the sheet around it a couple of times. Then flop into the cockpit. You will survive until somebody finds you or until you drift to shore. Remember, the the Sunfish evolved from a lifesaver's surfboard. It makes a pretty good life boat.

Clothing

Shorts and bare feet are the order of the day for most Sunfish sailing. You may as well get accustomed to getting wet. As it gets cooler—and even a hot day can be cool if you are wet and the wind is blowing—I usually add clothing from the waist up. I almost invariably wear a polo shirt with a life jacket over that, and usually a tee shirt over the life jacket. This keeps the jacket from snagging on the boom. If necessary, a foul-weather jacket comes next, covered by another tee shirt. If it is really cool, I wear a sweater beneath the foul-weather gear. Choose a wool sweater, for wool will keep you warm even if it is wet.

If, at the point I need a sweater, I'm starting to get cold from the waist down, I add foul-weather trousers to the costume. You will want the bib-type trousers or your back will be exposed when you are hiking out. Many sailors reverse the process, wearing bib-type foul-weather trousers before adding anything above the waist. This protects them from the wind, up to their armpits, at least—and, together with a life jacket, keeps most of the body warm. The arms are free to work the sheet and tiller. Whichever method suits you best, the important thing is to keep your trunk warm. If you do that, your arms and legs won't feel cold right away, and you'll be able to keep up your strength.

On a hot summer day, remember that you may be out on the water long enough to get quite a sunburn. If you are wearing a bathing suit or are shirtless, always take along a long-sleeved shirt and a bottle of suntan lotion. If you want to keep these items, or anything else, dry, put them in a really waterproof bag. We'll talk about some more esoteric items of clothing, pads and shoes, in a later section on racing.

3 *Tuning the Boat*

The concept of the Sunfish is to maintain a class that is as totally one-design as possible. Most of us believe that one can take a new Sunfish out of its box, assemble it, fiddle with the outhauls and the gooseneck a little, and go out and win a regatta. On the other hand, there are a lot of things you can do to your Sunfish that will, presumably, increase the odds in your favor. The class philosophy is to permit modifications that increase ease of sailing or safety, but not boat speed. Whether or not all the permitted modifications also give a slight racing edge, almost all the top Sunfish sailors take advantage of them.

● The Rudder

Two things can be done to the rudder blade. You can put on any kind of finish you want. You can do anything you want to the profile of the leading and trailing edges, so long as you don't go more than 1¼ inches in from the edges. This latter change was instituted by Alcort V. P. Bob Johnstone and, frankly, I do not believe it increases safety or ease of sailing. It just makes the boat faster. Changing the profile is, however, a lot of work. I personally wish the change hadn't been allowed.

A lot of sailors have studied the best possible airfoil section for the rudder, including studying the work of NACA. The usual technique is to sand down the trailing edge and build up the leading edge a little before sanding it to a roughly elliptical section. The objectives are twofold: to provide the fastest shape through the water; and to resist stalling out or cavitation as the rudder is angled to the water during steering maneuvers. Some sailors opt for the elliptical foil section. Others choose a more rounded leading edge on the theory that this resists stalling slightly better than a sharper leading edge.

In terms of finish, the consensus is that a fine, sanded surface is better than a very glossy one. I believe some test-tank work has been done on this. The factory finish on the wood parts of the Sunfish is glossy smooth, but follows the contours of the unfilled mahogany, leaving a slightly ridged effect. Sanding this finish down smooth will often expose raw wood, so that refinishing is probably a good idea, even if you don't doctor the leading and trailing edges.

Most sailors feel that rudder, tiller and tiller extension should all be one almost rigid unit, with as little slop and sideplay as possible. In time, the bolt on which the rudder pivots in the rudder cheeks loosens up, and a certain amount of play results. Paul Odegard discovered a source for stainless-steel bushings that can be used to take up this play; a few sailors will install them on a new rudder, just as preventive maintenance. Such repairs are accepted as being within class rules; Alcort published this fix in the class newspaper.

The second area for slop can develop between the rudder and the tiller. Normally, this can be controlled by insuring that the tiller bolt is kept quite tight. In time, however, the bushing treatment may be needed here, as well.

If you happen to get an older boat—quite a bit older, now—it may have the old-style rudder fitting, rather than the present spring-loaded, counterbalanced aluminum one. The old rudder

(Top) *According to class rules, the Sunfish rudder is legal if swept back at a 120-degree angle, but is illegal at 90 degrees.*

(Bottom left) *For a safe sure grip, wrap the tiller with twine or cover with leather. Be sure to cover the "ringding" with tape so it won't snag.*

(Bottom right) *To shape rudder, make a tracing of this full-size template (Courtesy Larry Cochran and Paul Odegard).*

45

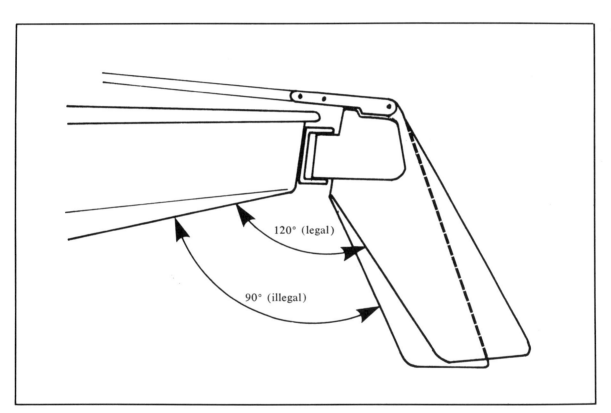

120° (legal)

90° (illegal)

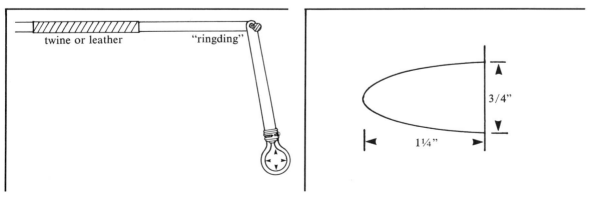

twine or leather   "ringding"

3/4"

1¼"

fitting swings on a bronze unit screwed to the deck and pivots down, snapping into a latch arrangement screwed into the bottom of the hull. The newer rudder fitting attaches to the hull by means of a stainless-steel bracket bolted to the transom. On the old-style fitting, the top and bottom fittings screw to the hull and are connected by a long bolt and wing nut. A heavy spring provides latch tension. When the rudder kicks up, it jumps out of the latch. This rig is not nearly as satisfactory as the present one. If one forgets to tighten the wing nut securely after seating the rudder, the rudder has a tendency to pop out when it sustains heavy loads, as when running before the wind in heavy weather. And when that happens, the boat rounds up like a car skidding on ice. In time, the latch arrangement wears down, and it is almost impossible to keep the rudder from popping out in heavy air. It is also possible to catch the rudder at the wrong angle, especially when beaching the boat, ripping the deck fitting right off the deck. In time, the single large screw holding the bottom fitting works its way out of the mahogany or oak block beneath the fiberglass, usually at the most inopportune time. Most sailors agree that the new unit is far superior, although at first some worried that it was heavier because of its massiveness. Weight at the ends of a boat is deplored, because it creates oscillations that can make the boat "hobbyhorse" through the water and impede its progress.

Many sailors provide some kind of anti-chafing material where the tiller rubs against the bridle. This can range from leather, to turns of light line, to duct tape. Such chafing gear, while not specifically allowed in the rules, is obviously intended to protect the boat and cannot in any way increase the speed. So, it has never been questioned. Up at the tip of the tiller, the bolt, nut, retaining pin and washers of the tiller extension or hiking stick should all be inspected from time to time, and will need adjustment fairly regularly to maintain the degree of friction preferred by the sailor. Some like this fitting fairly loose, so that it swivels easily. Others prefer it quite tight, so the tiller extension will stay in whatever position desired. In 1981, the rules were changed to permit a universal joint between tiller and extension. Some skippers, obviously, like the new proviso.

Because both tiller and extension are quite thin at the point where they are bolted together, they have a tendency to split, especially after a year or two of rough handling in racing conditions. When refinishing these two pieces of wood, it is a good idea to make sure that varnish or paint gets down into the bolt holes to protect them from eventually rotting. It's a good idea to refinish wood pieces while they are still brand new.

It is also a good idea, when you buy your Sunfish, to inspect both tiller and extension. The grain should be perfectly straight and parallel to the edges of both sticks. Angle grain breaks quite easily. More than one sailor has lost the tip of his tiller or hiking stick in the middle of a heavy-air race. It's almost impossible to hike out and steer with a broken tiller.

Class rules permit a handle on the tiller exten-

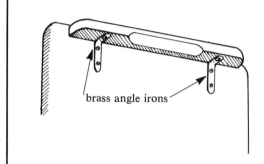

The daggerboard handles should be strengthened with brass angle irons trimmed short on top and set flush into the wood.

brass angle irons

47

sion, provided it does not exceed two inches in any dimension. This can be a two-inch wood or rubber ball, a brass ring or—most common—a standard Alcort sail clip. To install a sail clip, drill a hole on one side of the tiller extension for the prong of the sail clip and attach it firmly to the other side with a round or combination-head stainless-steel screw. Number 8 or 6, ½-inch, seems about right. Most sailors install the clip in a horizontal rather than vertical position. In the vertical position, the set will prevent the extension from slipping over the top of the tiller when tacking or jibing. The prong of the sail clip can be glued into the hole or held by a couple of brass tacks. Then the connection should be taped or lashed with light twine.

The Daggerboard

The daggerboard should be shaped and refinished in the same manner as the rudder. The only additional comment I can think of is that the two strips of wood across the top, which serve as stops to prevent the board from falling through the hull, almost always tear loose by splitting the board where the screws are fastened. This happens when you slam the board down harder than you mean to, because the adrenaline is pumping as you come down on the leeward mark. For years now, I have installed small brass angle irons under these stops, and extended the life of a board to 10 years or more. It also helps to remove the screws and apply a little epoxy before screwing them back down again.

Under the class rules, installation of a handle

or eye on top of the daggerboard is permitted. This helps raise the board and also permits a line to be fastened so the board won't be lost overboard. Usually, the other end of the line is fastened to the halyard cleat, or around the mast. For the last couple of years, Alcort has drilled a hole through one of the daggerboard stops and installed a padeye on deck, forward of the slot. The daggerboard line can be fastened to these if desired. I have only lost one daggerboard in 16 years of Sunfish racing so I don't bother with the line. To me, it is just one more line to get tangled in something.

Another item specifically permitted by the rules is a daggerboard-retaining device. The design that is used almost universally today encircles the board with a length of shock cord held in tension across the deck by loops of line and hooks over the deck edge on either side. The loop rides around the forward and after edges of the daggerboard, and provides a snubbing action that keeps the board at whatever position it is raised to. Since the snubbing action is equal both fore and aft, the edges are not rubbed against the daggerboard trunk, which can crush the fibers and eventually peel off little feathers of mahogany that really slow the boat down. Originally, most sailors used a length of shock cord looped around the trailing edge of the daggerboard and fastened to the mast. This served the purpose quite adequately, but did, in time, create those feathers.

Another form of daggerboard-retaining device that I saw in the early '60s, but not since, was a pair of the spring-loaded rollers that were once sold for controlling window rattles in automobiles. They are mounted on the deck, one on the forward edge of the daggerboard trunk and one on the after edge. These provided enough friction to hold the board in the position desired and also held the board away from the sharp edges of the trunk. However, they did not last very long, since they were made of a steel that had no resistance to rusting. I haven't seen these used for many years. The concept, however, makes sense.

A third type of daggerboard-retaining device, one that I tried for years to get incorporated into the rules, is a combination of shock cord and line—or just shock cord, if you don't mind spending the money—that goes from the tack, where upper and lower spar meet, around the mast, around the back of the daggerboard, back around the mast and halyard, and fastens on the other end to the tack. This set-up serves two purposes, as a daggerboard retainer and a JC strap.

The JC strap pulls the boom outboard automatically when you let the sheet off—very handy when you are rounding the windward mark in very light air and the wind isn't strong enough to push it up against the friction of the spars on the mast and the mast in the mast hole. During critical roundings, it is nice to be able to use your hands for raising the daggerboard, steering, and handling the sheet. Since this rig doesn't cost any more than any other sort of snubbing device, the rule was finally changed to permit it. Actually, it had been used for a couple of years in the late '60s within the rules, but then the rule was changed to outlaw it. I have never been able to fathom why.

Daggerboard sections: (1) The ideal airfoil section won't fit in the well (dotted line). However, the standard board's cross-section (2) may be built up with auto body putty or Marinetex and then rounded to an elliptical shape on the leading edge (3). The completed board may be covered with fiberglass cloth and resin.

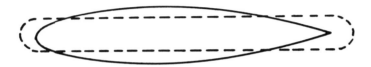

1. *Ideal airfoil.*

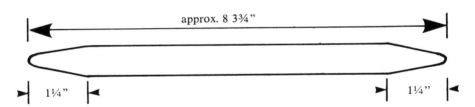

approx. 8 3¾"

1¼"   1¼"

2. *Standard cross-section.*

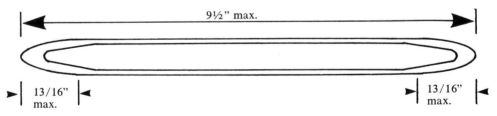

9½" max.

13/16"
max.   13/16"
max.

3. *Improved cross-section.*

This rig has the drawback of pulling the board forward, but a piece of shock cord tight across the front of the daggerboard from one side of the deck to the other and a little care in raising and lowering helps preserve the board for many seasons.

● The Bridle

A lot of thought has gone into various methods of overriding the function of the bridle, which is merely to hold the end of the sheet centered over the tiller. Why the interest? On the Sunfish, the sail is set on the port side of the mast and the boom is also off-center by about six inches. The sail sets differently on port tack than on starboard. The theory is that, because the bridle and the forward sheet hook are on the centerline, the set of the sail differs and that the sail is fuller on starboard tack because the mast does not cut into it.

Garry Hoyt, the first Sunfish World Champion, theorized that there is also less tension on the leech while on starboard tack, since there is less downward force on the boom. The angle from the deck plane is slightly more acute because of the off-center boom. He and a lot of other sailors in the Caribbean began attaching the sheet clip to the left half of the bridle to compensate for this off-center position and the greater power derived on starboard tack.

Over the years, many Caribbean Sunfish racers have decided that the sheet should be allowed to slide along the bridle on both starboard and port tacks. To accomplish this, they tie a loose bowline instead of using the sister hooks. Even so, the loop of the line will usually hang up under the bridle eye, and must be shoved by foot or hand to the leeward position. So, many sailors began taking a number of turns of tape around the bridle eye, providing a smoother path for the sheet loop to follow.

This adjustment was not permitted at the Worlds until 1978. In 1980, the rules were further relaxed to permit a piece of line to be substituted for the bridle. It can be knotted to curtail the sheet's travel as much as desired on either tack but must be between 30 and 32 inches long.

It is also legal to use any length sheet, and to tie the sheet's end to the bridle in any way you wish. The consensus seems to be that the boat sails best in light air with the sheet tied or clipped to the bridle loop. But in heavy air, one of the systems that allows the sheet end to slide to leeward on starboard and port tacks is generally favored.

Quite by accident, I discovered what I believed to be the ideal position for the sheet end. The port loop on my bridle, where it fastens to the deck through the padeye, broke. I formed a new loop on the shortened bridle and taped the loop tightly. With this repair, I had a shorter bridle with the center loop a couple of inches left of the centerline. This seemed to work slightly better in all kinds of weather— so well, in fact, that I began to wonder about its legality. I checked with the class secretary at the 1980 Worlds. He ruled it legal. Still, the now-legal rope bridle is best of all because it is fully adjustable.

When the Sunfish jibes, it is not unusual for the sheet to droop down from the boom and

The shape of the Sunfish sail is affected by the boat's off-center boom.

The bridle. Performance may be improved by adding limit knots to the bridle. The rope bridle is best because it's adjustable.

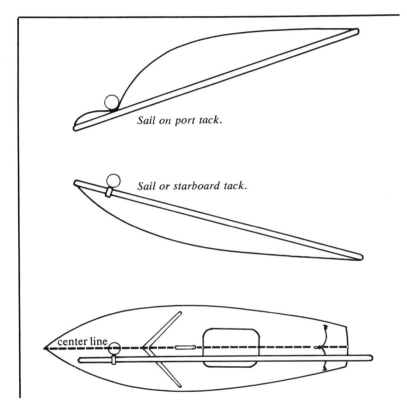

Sail on port tack.

Sail or starboard tack.

center line

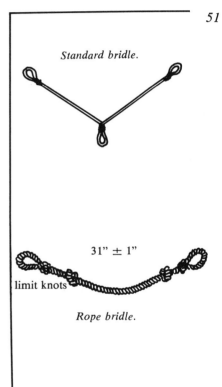

Standard bridle.

31" ± 1"

limit knots

Rope bridle.

catch an ear or life jacket. Provide a loop of something soft on the boom over the cockpit to prevent this. Use a loop of tape, line, or a length of hose. You might not mind losing an ear, but you surely don't want to capsize!

● The Cockpit

Some people put antiskid striping on the side decks along the cockpit and on the bottom of the cockpit itself. Most racers, however, find they want to slide back and forth rather than anchor themselves in one position. If you have an older Sunfish, the inside lip of the cockpit may not have an aluminum protective strip. This strip, which has been installed for the last 10 years or so, is a mixed blessing. It protects the raw fiberglass edge from your shoes and you from any sharp edges of fiberglass, but on occasion the rivets that hold the strip work loose, leaving sharp projections to snag your clothing or skin. Some owners tape this edge all the way around the cockpit, or even install a split piece of rubber hose or surgical tubing to protect their feet while hiking out. Again, while not specifically permitted by the rules, the adjustment is not likely to get anyone very excited.

In heavy weather, a lot of water sweeps across the decks. The fewer obstructions, the better. A coaming or splash rail really acts as a brake when you take a lot of water over the bow, but it is illegal to remove the Sunfish coaming. It does deflect water from you and the cockpit which, by the way, is a most effective brake itself, not to mention a water trap. If your bailer isn't working—or even if it is—you're likely to be sailing with three or four inches of water in the cockpit in heavy weather.

There might be an advantage to decking over the cockpit completely but that would probably be disallowed. In one Connecticut River race, I stowed all our gear in the cockpit, covered with a tarpaulin. The idea was not so much to avoid shipping water as to provide better weight distribution and allow me to carry the sail closer to the deck. Whatever I gained that way, however, I lost in ease of handling, and we also managed to ship a little water, which made for wet sleeping bags. Since then, I have gone back to the original system of carrying our gear in several heavy-duty plastic garbage bags strapped to the deck around the mast.

● Sheet Blocks

Probably the first pieces of additional equipment a sailor will install on a Sunfish are a deck-mounted mainsheet block and mainsheet cleats. The simplest rig is just a swivelling block with an integral cam cleat, but most racers find this unsatisfactory. When hiking out hard, you cannot always release the sheet from the cam cleat without pulling yourself part way back into the boat to get the right angle. Since you are normally trying to release the sheet when a puff hits, you also want to be hiked out as far as you can. Coming back into the boat allows the boat to heel and, in extreme conditions, can cause capsize. Most sailors prefer a block centered on deck right in front of the mainsheet hook, and vertical clam cleats as far outboard as the configuration of the deck over the cockpit will permit. Depending on the

Sunfish deck layout. A place for everything and everything in its place.

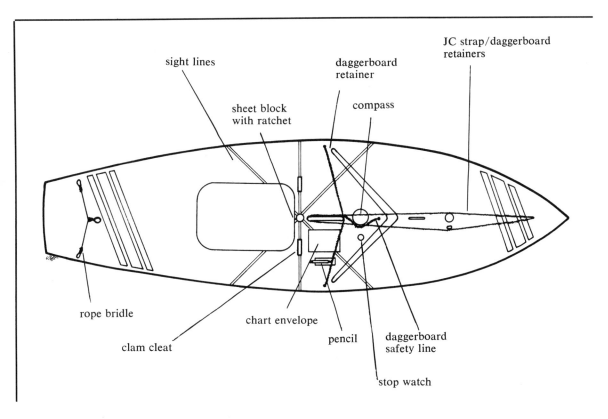

sight lines

daggerboard retainer

JC strap/daggerboard retainers

sheet block with ratchet

compass

rope bridle

clam cleat

chart envelope

pencil

daggerboard safety line

stop watch

block used, you may want to raise the cleat on blocks of wood to give them the proper bite on the line as it comes out of the block.

Some owners actually raise the cleats on wooden blocks two or three inches high to provide a hand-hold. On long windward legs like those at the Worlds, the hand-hold offers an opportunity to rest a little while hiking hard, by taking some of the strain off the legs. I have accomplished the same thing at the Worlds by using longer bolts and stacks of washers beneath the cleats. For me, this is more comfortable than the wood block arrangement.

● The Foredeck

Between the forward edge of the cockpit and the splash rail, lots of interesting things can sprout up aboard a Sunfish. We used to call the foredeck of Carl Knight's boat his flight deck! He had put down strips of tape as sight lines for measuring various tactical conditions. He had one strip at 90 degrees to the centerline of the boat to help him determine when a competitor's mast was abeam, or when he had reached the lay line on a beat. From the center of this strip, he had two more strips of tape angled forward at 45 degrees. These helped him determine whether a boat on the opposite tack would clear or whether a collision was imminent. On the afterdeck, he had extensions of these 45-degree lines to help him tell when he could tack and clear a boat to weather. On the "flight deck," he also installed a protractor arrangement with which he kept track of the compass courses to each mark and the average compass readings on each tack. I have a hunch

that he needed this very seldom, and kept it there primarily as a "psych."

● The Compass

Most Sunfish racers mount a compass in a wooden box that can then be strapped to the deck with shock cord or taped down with that most important item in the sailor's ditty bag— duct tape. (Use the latter to patch a sail, protect the gooseneck from the boom, the deck from the eyebolt, whip a line, hold racing instructions to the deck beneath clear plastic, etc., etc.)

A compass is important for helping you detect wind shifts when there is no good reference point like a buoy or shoreline with prominent features. It can also help you find the next mark on long courses. Many sailors who race only on small lakes or protected harbors find the compass unnecessary, but if you travel to major regattas on large bodies of water, you will need one.

The quality of the compass is important. I have made do with an Airex compass of the type sold by AMF Alcort. They used to cost just over $10, complete with a mounting bracket, and now probably cost twice that. But it is not unheard of for a sailor to spend $100 for a good Suunto or Danforth compass, which holds its position better on a bouncing deck. I remember Paul Fendler giving credit for his win at the 1975 Worlds in Venezuela to his compass. He said it allowed him to detect five-degree wind shifts, which he played on every windward leg.

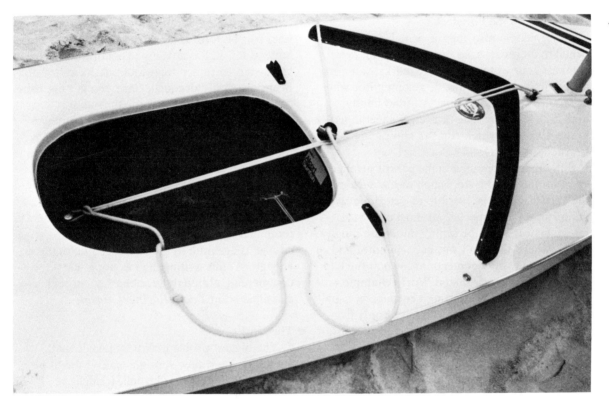

A legal set of hiking straps
for very short people—the halyard
carried around the old-style metal
bailer and back up to the halyard
cleat, very taut. This won't work
with the new plastic bailer.

Many people also tape a pencil or grease pencil to their decks, so that they can jot down compass courses to each of the marks, sail numbers of major competitors or a competitor who has fouled them, and so on. Another handy item is a clear vinyl bag or acetate sheet taped to the deck into which you can slip racing instructions or a section of a chart.

Still other sailors have some sort of arrangement for fastening a stopwatch to the deck or the splash rail. It is possible to get along without a stopwatch, especially if most of the starting sequences you'll be sailing under are dinghy starts, where they call out each minute, and have a second-by-second countdown at the end. But at North American and World championships, official IYRU starting sequence is usually used, in which you receive signals at only five-minute intervals. Even under these conditions, you may be able to operate without a stopwatch. I can usually get by with the sweep second hand on my regular watch; I have trained myself to note its position at the warning signal, and keep track of the time that way.

I have had bad luck with stopwatches; none of mine have ever proved themselves waterproof. I figure that it has cost me about $5 per start, going through three different stopwatches. On the other hand, with the red sweep-second hand of my trusty Timex, I can do just as well (if not better—sometimes I thought I had clicked the button on the stopwatch and found that it had not started). However, most serious racers consider a stopwatch indispensable.

Another word about stopwatches—Jumper Lee, son of John Black Lee, the father of the Super Sunfish, has developed a stopwatch you listen to rather than look at. Its series of beeps are easily decoded, once you get the hang of it. Thus, you can know the time almost continuously, and don't have to take your eyes off the competition and the starting line. I like the idea. In fact, I once called out the time into a little pocket dictating machine, rewound it, and then timed it as it played back. Unfortunately, it was off by three or four seconds in the five-minute countdown, and that is much too much of an error. Jumper's gadget, of course, is accurate to the microsecond, or close enough. At this writing, he has not gone commercial, although he sold a few through a classified ad in *Yacht Racing/Cruising*.

● **The Hull**

The biggest problem with Sunfish is that, sooner or later, they spring a leak. It might be around the daggerboard trunk, it might be around the mast step, it might be around the bailer, or it might be where the hull joins the deck. You might even get a wicking effect through the fiberglass from minor cracks in the gelcoat. As soon as that happens, you will probably get an added five or 10 pounds of weight to your boat, just from water absorbed through the hull. Of course, the longer you are on the water during a race, the more that leak will fill you up. It's not just the weight of the water. It's more the sloshing of the water back and forth, creating oscillations that will slow you down, especially as you try to work your way through waves. At this point, if he has not already put one in as a matter of convenience, the sailor will probably install one or more hatches. That way, he can get into the hull with a sponge and get out the loose water. Transom-mounted plugs on either side of the rudder can also be used. The tiny plug Alcort installs on the starboard edge of the deck does not do the job very effectively.

A number of Sunfish owners have installed hatches fore and aft on the deck. They then blow hot air through the hull using the blowing end of a canister vacuum cleaner. After a few hours, the hull will be considerably lighter, as the warm air hauls the dampness out of the fiberglass. Class rules permit ports, but they are not supposed to be opened during a race. I have one in the center of my deck, just forward of the daggerboard trunk, and I will usually sponge the boat as dry as I can between races. There is some disagreement as to whether this is permitted between races while one is still out on the water, or whether the boat has to be taken to shore to be bailed. I lean towards the first interpretation.

Serious racers often debate the subject of hull weight versus hull stiffness. Sometimes a light hull is important but, given the choice, I prefer a stiff, somewhat heavier hull. A light hull means that you will get on a plane a little sooner, and in lighter wind. But stiffness will help your boat speed both on and off the wind. Furthermore, it is the current consensus among dinghy racers that a hull so light that it works as it goes through the waves slows you down.

I suppose one should strive for as light a hull as possible without compromising stiffness. I don't know anything that can be done to stiffen a hull, unless it is to apply another layer of fiberglass. That might be considered legal, since any type of coating may be applied to the hull, rudder or board. Whether my argument in favor of stiffness would apply with so much additional weight, I cannot guess. Of course, you might go a step further, and apply some longitudinal carbon-fiber stiffening to the outside of the hull, but I suspect that would be against the spirit, if not the letter, of the rules.

We'll talk more about this matter of stiffness versus light weight later, in conversations with 1981 National Champion Paul Odegard and two-time World Champion Derrick Fries.

4 *Tuning the Rig*

(Facing page, top) *The halyard and gooseneck should be adjusted according to wind conditions. Left to right: day sailing, light air racing, heavy air racing, "Jens Hookansen" heavy air racing.*

(Facing page, bottom) *The Jens or Hookansen rig: mast and boom secured by a knot for heavy air sailing. Use the halyard or, preferably, a separate line to make the knot.*

58 The most important part of tuning, other than modifications to the board and rudder, involves the sail and spars. When set up as recommended by AMF Alcort literature that comes with each boat, the rig is not very efficient for racing. The first thing that must be done is to lower the rig by tying the halyard at least one full sail clip higher on the upper spar. This will bring the boom close down to the deck. Most successful racers carry their boom so that the tack is roughly two inches off the deck. We would carry them even closer, but halyards do stretch and slip. If the tack drops onto the deck, the ever-present danger of gouging a semicircular track materializes. The accompanying sketches show ways to protect the deck.

● The Gooseneck

The gooseneck can slide fore and aft but the factory position is too far aft if you lower the rig. Most racers move the gooseneck forward. Most like to adjust it according to wind conditions, moving it forward in light air—as close as 12 inches from the tack—and aft as the wind picks up. In very heavy air, the boom will be carried almost parallel with the deck; in light air, it will be cocked up towards the stern quite markedly. The consensus on the location of the gooseneck seems to be about 14 inches from the tack.

When adjusting the gooseneck constantly, it does not take long to strip the bronze machine screw that secures the fitting. Carl Knight had a stainless-steel Allen screw in his gooseneck, and a number of others have followed suit. The Allen screw is easier to turn than a standard

screw and an Allen wrench is easier to carry than a screwdriver. At the 1980 Worlds, AMF's Steve Baker handed out stainless-steel bolts, which worked fine.

● The Jens Rig

Another approach to the gooseneck position question is to tie the halyard off on the upper spar at approximately the factory-recommended position, and then to tie the upper spar to the mast about 12 or 18 inches below the mast peak. This was first popularized by Jens Hookansen of the Virgin Islands, who won the North Americans with it in 1976 at Association Island. The purpose of this complicated procedure, called a Jens or Hookansen rig, is to make the upper spar bendier, so that it will sag off in heavy air, flattening the sail and spilling wind from the peak. This, in turn, makes it easier to hold the boat flat, so the boat sails faster, even though the sail is now less efficient. In other words, even the Sunfish sail can overpower the boat when the wind gets strong enough.

An obvious answer to the cumbersome Jens rig would be to cut 12 or 16 inches off the bottom of the mast, eliminating the necessity to tie off the upper spar. As far as I know, nobody has tried this yet. It would probably be ruled illegal. Of course, masts do break from time to time. Dave Chapin's broke at the 1978 North Americans. He just stuck the broken mast back into the boat, tied the halyard lower on the upper spar, and sailed off. He won the next race that way, but had to switch back to a complete mast for the rest of the series.

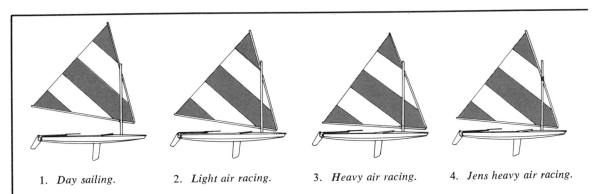

1. *Day sailing.*   2. *Light air racing.*   3. *Heavy air racing.*   4. *Jens heavy air racing.*

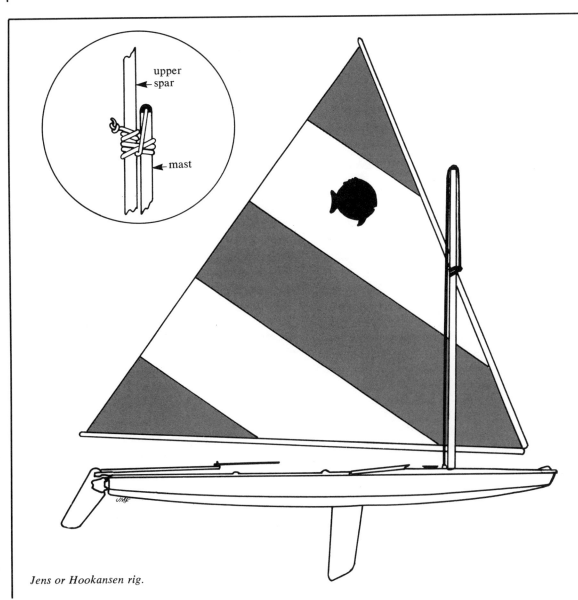

upper
← spar

←mast

Jens or Hookansen rig.

Jens Hookansen of St. Croix (40) the year he won the North Americans in heavy air with his now-famous "Jens rig"—the upper spar tied low on the mast. Note, also, his hiking technique. His right foot is under the cockpit lip, with his left crossed over it and hooked under the boom. He claimed it was comfortable!

60

There was a move afoot to ban the Hookansen rig on the grounds that it prevented the sail from being lowered fully. I can certainly imagine a black squall hitting a fleet and capsizing everybody. Some might then want to lower their sail in the water, right the boat, and ride out the storm that way. In fact, the Jens rig makes it very difficult to lower the sail. One solution that has just recently been allowed is to tie the Jens with a separate loop of line. Don't tie the loop too tightly or it may prevent the sail from dropping, even with the halyard slacked off. A more elegant solution would be to permit the installation of a sleeve through the mast. The halyard could be fed through this at the desired Jens position. Or the rules could allow masts of different heights, with maybe a maximum of three masts—one for the standard rig, another, 12 inches shorter, for heavy air, and one 18 inches shorter for survival conditions.

Bending on the Sail

Setting the sail on the spars is another highly important aspect of tuning. After 1967, when the new, fuller-cut sail was introduced, it was important to set these sails very loosely on the spars. Bending on the sail this way produces a pronounced scallop along the foot, and often a bit of a scallop along the luff as well. I will not put up with a sail that must be set slightly scalloped along the luff, since the scalloping starts to flutter a little before normal luffing, and, I believe, requires footing off just a hair more than a sail that can be set with a little tautness along the luff. Most other sailors,

Ways to lace lines when bending sail to spar. Nylon clips can also be used.

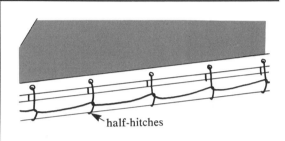

half-hitches

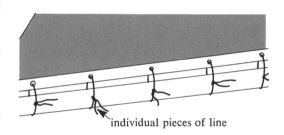

individual pieces of line

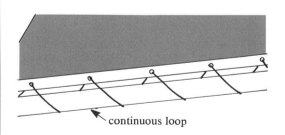

continuous loop

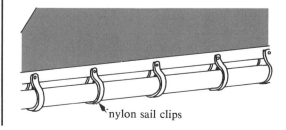

nylon sail clips

however, are not bothered by the slight amount of scallop sometimes required. The problem is not as severe with the new Fogh-designed sail, most sailors have found. It can be set quite taut.

Many sailors experiment with changes in foot and luff tension, in an attempt to provide different shapes for different wind conditions. Others experiment until they find "the best" set, and leave it there. However, as the competition has increased over the years, fiddling with outhauls has become the rule rather than the exception, and the class finally permitted adjustable outhauls in 1978. It is now permissible to install small cleats on both spars, with long lengths of line out to the ends of the spars and back to the tack and peak of the sails. With such a setup, the foot can be tightened and loosened right from the cockpit, while the luff can be tightened by stepping up on to the deck at the mast. I use the system, but I am not convinced that it is that important. However, it beats dropping the sails and leaning way out over the transom to adjust small lengths of line at the tips of the spars. For those who believe in adjustability, it is a safety and convenience feature.

The subject of sail clips versus lace line was a hot one up until about 15 years ago. This was partly because the sail was flatter, and sailors went to great lengths to try to get a little extra draft. Not much seemed to help, however. Some sailors laced the sail loosely at the clew, peak, and even tack, while others laced them tightly there but loosely in the middle of the foot and luff. For several years, I used sail sets on the luff and halfway up the foot, with lace lines from the aft end of the cockpit to the clew. This was more a matter of necessity than design, since I ran out of sail sets at one point. The boat seemed to move well that way, so I never changed it. It used to bug other competitors in the class; they thought I knew something they didn't. At that time, I also kept the foot and luff quite tight, until the sail finally stretched right to the very ends of the spars. Again, in those days, it seemed to work, since everybody had a flat sail anyway, and mine stretched out to a larger projected area for the runs, perhaps giving me an additional eyelash of speed.

● **The Free End of the Halyard**

The free end of the halyard is used for a great number of things, most of them considered legal. It can be tied to the tack, and then looped on deck around the mast with one loop on either side of it. On reaches and runs, the free end of the halyard can then be held taut, acting as a JC strap to hold the sail out. In heavy weather areas of the country and in the Caribbean many sailors use the end of the halyard to act as a downhaul on the gooseneck, to prevent the boom from riding up and thereby creating too much twist. Others will arrange some sort of a vang from the base of the mast to a point a foot or two aft of the gooseneck. I have used the JC-strap arrangement in light air, but now that the shock-cord/daggerboard-retaining-device/JC-strap arrangement is legal, I prefer to coil the halyard in small loops and jam it under the section from the padeye to the cleat. I use the downhaul arrangement in very heavy air.

Outhaul adjustments are readily
made with the aid of an easily
rigged two-to-one purchase as shown
here in both side and top views.

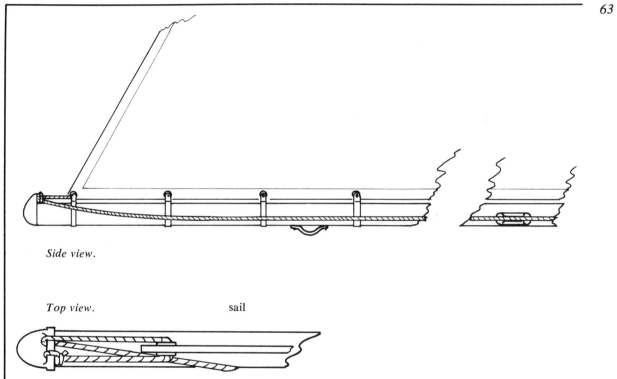

Side view.

Top view.   sail

*Woollies attached on **either** side of the sail are probably more confusing than helpful aboard a Sunfish. The masthead fly is equally superfluous. A peak fly, however, is needed for downwind sailing. Various types have been tried but those attached to a forward-facing V device seem best. Leech or trailing edge telltales may also be used.*

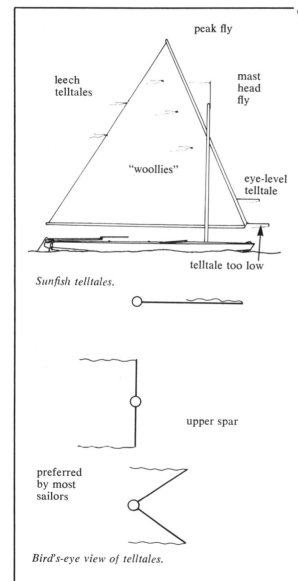

peak fly

leech telltales

mast head fly

"woollies"

eye-level telltale

telltale too low

Sunfish telltales.

upper spar

preferred by most sailors

Bird's-eye view of telltales.

● **Telltales**

In my opinion, you practically *have* to have telltales—not only a masthead fly, but a couple of yarns or feathers sticking out in front of the upper spar. Some people use only one, sticking straight out on a wire roughly parallel to the boom. Others carry two telltales on a straight piece of wire at 90 degrees to the boom. I prefer two telltales on wires at 90-degree angles to each other, each at a 45-degree angle to the boom. Such a telltale unit is available as the Feathermate, originally made by Paul Odegard and still sold commercially. It is fastened to the boom with a plastic clip and comes with both feathers and yarns, to suit your preference. I make mine from aluminum wire used to ground TV antennas. It can be bent and adjusted easily, and then folded out of the way when you roll up the sail.

There are dozens of commercial masthead flies available. But again, I prefer a piece of aluminum groundwire with a piece of yarn on the end, taped to the peak and sticking straight out like an extension of the upper spar. The main value of the masthead fly is for downwind work, but, under shifty conditions, especially in light air, it can help you deduce an average of winds coming at different angles. Yes, especially on small lakes and rivers, it is quite possible to have the wind abeam down at deck level and coming from straight ahead up at the fly, or vice versa. Knowing this, and adjusting your sail to the best average, can keep you moving while the rest of the boats are stalled out, and that can mean the difference between being in the pack or way out ahead. I know few sailors who can do that without telltales, and while such conditions are the exception, I use my telltales all the time, just in case.

In very heavy air, I find that the masthead fly is a better indicator than the eye-level flies. Why, I don't know. In very light air, I find myself concentrating almost exclusively on those forward, eye-level telltales, to take advantage of every wind shift. This is especially true if the wind is fairly evenly spread over the race course. On the other hand, especially in light-air conditions, it is quite likely that there will be a puff here and a puff there, with holes in between. When that happens, it is more important to keep your eye out for those telltale ruffles on the water, and try to sail into them, even if you are not always sailing on a lift.

In addition to telltales at the peak and at eye level, some sailors use a number of telltales on the sail itself. These are often called "woollies" to differentiate them from the ones out in free air. The idea is to fasten them on the sail along the foot and the luff, or aft of the mast, one on each side, in pairs. When airflow is optimum, the windward woollies should stream aft and the leeward ones should actually lift above horizontal. In addition, many sailors use telltales on the leech of the sail. They are supposed to stream aft when the airflow is optimum. My new Fogh sail came with a leech "woolly" attached, and two sets each for the sail surface itself. I have always thought "woollies" were superfluous on a Sunfish sail, and have not learned to use them successfully on other class sails either. My opinion seems to be shared by most of the top Sunfish sailors, who believe that the turbulence caused by the sail clips and the mast renders such "woollies" useless. Most other classes, however, swear by them.

5 *Tuning You*

We've talked about tuning your boat. Now, if you really want to be in the top ranks of competition, you have to be in good tune yourself. These days, most Olympic yachtsmen train for their sport as intensively as a track star. They run. They lift weights. They even study ballet.

For Sunfish racing, the two most important sets of muscles are your hiking muscles and your sheet-pulling muscles.

● Hiking Muscles

Your hiking muscles are mostly leg and back muscles. For a while, some Sunfish sailors concentrated on their stomach muscles. In fact, these are not vital in hiking. In a proper hiking position, you are sitting upright, with your tail out over the water. Your weight is supported by your legs, with lots of pressure under your thighs, somewhere between your bottom and your knees. Since your center of gravity is somewhere around your waist, leaning back while you are hiked out adds relatively little righting moment. You will lean way back for momentary surges of wind, but it is impossible for even the best-trained athletes to sail a half-hour windward leg in a prone hiked-out position. Some sailors sail light-air races with their backs on the side deck, so they can keep their profile low and their eyes on the sail. There is no strain on the leg or stomach muscles in that position, but your neck will get stiff.

Training muscles to hold a tense position, resisting considerable force, requires somewhat different conditioning than would be required for repetitive movements. Paul Elvström, who invented many of today's dinghy-racing techniques, had a special bench from which he could hike out while sitting at his desk. The best exercise for developing hiking muscles is hiking out!

You can get much the same effect with an exercise suggested by Larry Lewis. Stand with your back about one to two feet away from a wall. Then lean back against the wall, bending your knees so that your thighs are roughly horizontal to the ground. If you are not used to it, this exercise will bring tears to your eyes in a few minutes. But, after a while, you should be able to hold it for 30 minutes or so and catch up on your reading at the same time. I would suggest shifting your position a little, once in a while, while you are doing this, or you may cut off your circulation.

As many a sufferer knows, the back is one of the most vulnerable parts of the human anatomy. Long periods of hiking out while pulling against the sheet and tiller can put a lot of strain on your back. So, back-limbering exercises are a good idea. The old stand-by, touching your toes, is good. Lying on your back and pulling your knees up to your chest—one at a time, and then both together—is also good. When you have done that for a while, clasp your knees with your arms and rock back and forth. Start these exercises slowly, working up your intensity of exertion carefully, since back muscles need to be limbered up before they can safely do their best work. I don't mean to ignore sit-ups, but they have been over-emphasized.

● Sheeting Muscles

To get your arm and shoulder muscles in cor-

Joel Furman, North American Champion in 1975, demonstrates the spread-eagle hiking style favored by short people.

rect shape, you can use various hand weights and pulling machines. The motion you will be using most consistently while sailing is pulling the sheet from the block or deck hook position to shoulder height—and even over your head, if you are pumping the sail hard to get on a plane. So, simulating the same sort of motion with a weight or weighted line on a pulley arrangement is a good exercise. Of course, if you can substitute sailing regularly in heavy air for these exercises, you will work all the proper muscles and have fun at the same time.

I have from time to time considered setting up a Sunfish, or a simulation of its deck area, on some sort of motorized gadget that will simulate a stiff chop, something like the bucking-bronco machines that are popular these days in "Western" bars. There would be a block on deck with a 5/16th-inch line reeved through to a pair of overhead pulleys. Suspend a 10- or 15-pound weight from the line and you would simulate as nearly as possible actual sailing conditions. Even without the bucking arrangement, such a rig would be worthwhile. Hike out and pump the sheet for an hour every other day and you should be able to survive any regatta without tiring. Tired sailors don't sail fast.

Pads

Hiking out hard on a Sunfish can cause pain. If you hike with the natural crease between your buttocks and thighs at the edge of the boat, you're not hiking hard enough in heavy air. You have to go beyond that. And for every inch beyond, the leverage of your body increases, squeezing the backs of your legs against hard fiberglass.

To spread out the pressure a little, many sailors sew pieces of heavy carpet to the backs of their sailing pants. Others wear two or three pairs of sweat pants. I tried the foam pads from an old life jacket slipped into special pockets on the legs of some coveralls. Very comfortable, but it made ducking under the boom when tacking chancy at best. After a couple of capsizes, I took out the pads and accepted the discomfort. Upside down is slow, too!

● **Shoes**

I usually sail barefoot, and my toes have paid for it over the years. Some sailors wear Topsiders, others wear tennis or basketball sneakers, and still others sea boots or special French-made hiking shoes. If you have cleats bolted through the foredeck into the cockpit, you'll be especially smart to protect your feet. Even more dangerous than cleat bolts in the cockpit are hazards on shore: broken bottles and the ringdings from pop-open cans, or clam shells, broken bits of concrete or more exotic hazards like coral. All those and more have bitten friends of mine who were launching Sunfish.

Other things to guard or pad yourself against: the boom block that grabs your hair; the many hard corners that can smack your knees or elbows. Think about wearing a sweatband or hat, together with basketball kneepads and elbow pads.

● **Carrying Weight**

The ideal Sunfish sailor would be about seven feet tall and weigh 145 pounds. He would have massive shoulders and most of his weight in the chest area, and would never tire. As far as I know, there is no Sunfish sailor who meets this description, and that is just as well. He would probably be unbeatable, if his sailing skills were really good. An individual with such a physical description would be light enough to get his boat on a plane quickly even in marginal conditions, and could get his weight outboard to hold the boat down in very strong puffs. With the weight high, he would also be able to get his body moving with the pendulum effect used by many top sailors to torque their boats over the waves to windward, or to "ooch" on a wave to get it planing off the wind.

There are no Sunfish sailors of quite this description, but most of the top ones come close, either naturally or with the help of extra weight. Derrick Fries, for instance, is a little heavier than the ideal, but he has a long limber body and great strength. Dave Chapin and Cor van Aanholt are light, but carry enough extra weight on their shoulders to give them that hiking and pendulum ability.

The only weight allowed is water. This is carried either in the form of wet clothing or in rubber bottles on chest and back. The reasoning is that, if you fall overboard, the water will not pull you down, since it weighs as much as the stuff you're floating in. If you are wearing the life jacket required by Sunfish rules when carrying extra weight, you won't drown. However, the wet clothing or the water bottles should be easily removable. Otherwise you will find it very difficult to climb back into the boat. Dave swears by water bottles; Cor hates water bottles, but swears by cotton sweatshirts.

You can buy special water jackets, such as the one Dave Chapin wears, or you can get cotton sweat shirts and soak them up. Most people who use sweats tear off the sleeves and slit them down the front, cardigan fashion, with some kind of simple release arrangement to hold them together. Then, if you fall in, you can take them off easily.

Carried high on the chest and back, weight can be leveraged fully for hiking out and for torquing. You don't need very much. Ten or 15 pounds seem to be plenty for even the well-conditioned athlete. If you do wear extra weight, remember that the Sunfish class limit is 10 kilos, or 22.2 pounds, as of the 1980 class rules. (The IYRU permits up to 22 kilos —almost 50 pounds—of wet clothing, and some of the early Finn sailors tried to carry that much to match the muscular gorillas who seem to gravitate to that man-killing class. As a result, not a few Finn sailors have bad backs. A bad back, as everyone who has ever had even a touch of back problem will tell you, is no fun.)

Unless you are in good shape and keep your back limber, you are probably better off not wearing any sort of weight. In the first place, it is more important to be alert and fresh than to be heavy. All the weight in the world won't help if your mind is foggy and your reflexes have gone numb from the exertion of carrying too much weight.

Unless you are sure you can handle the extra weight around your upper torso, consider wear-ing a couple of pairs of terry cloth shorts. If you are hiking properly with your rear end well outboard, that will help hold the boat down without putting extra strain on your back. That's Paul Odegard's technique, and he is no slouch to windward in heavy air.

6 *The Start and the Windward Leg*

It is impossible to reach the top ranks of racing without knowing instinctively the International Yacht Racing Union rules under which you will be competing. Most of the rules are quickly and easily understood and, for convenience, can be abbreviated on 4x5-inch cards. The United States Yacht Racing Union (USYRU) publishes a fine capsule summary of the rules prepared by Tom Ehman, three-time runner-up at the Sunfish North Americans. The rulebook itself is also available from USYRU as are a number of books explaining and picturing how the rules work in practice.

Scattered among the race situations described in the following pages are tactical situations involving the rules. Study these and Eric Twiname's *The Rules Book* together with the abbreviated rules so that you understand how the rules apply. Expect to get lots of education from race post-mortems, too. Unless you are very cautious, you are certain to become personally involved in a few protest hearings as well. When you do, conduct yourself in a gentlemanly fashion.

I think a word about the *spirit* of the rules is in order here. Until recently, and even then only in major regattas, there were no umpires or judges on the course. Every sailor was considered to be honest and willing voluntarily to take his medicine if he caused a foul. When there was a legitimate disagreement, a protest was in order. This code of honor is called "Corinthianism." I think it is too bad that we seldom hear the word anymore. As far as I'm concerned, winning is not the only thing. The competition, the fun, the good times with friends are the important things. I know that most Sunfish sailors agree with me.

One final point on the rules: Until you are confident about the rules, play it safe and stay out of the way. The sailor who causes a flagrant foul at a multiboat mark rounding can ruin a regatta for several others who might otherwise have been in contention. Of course, if you foul someone and damage his boat, the honest thing to do is pay for repairs. I am constantly amazed at the number of times a new sailor will crash into another competitor, holing the other's hull or tearing a sail, and then slip off never to be seen again. I assume they do this out of shame, not dishonesty, but the effect is the same.

● The Start

Almost all sailboat races begin with a timed start and each sailor's objective is to be sailing full speed with clear air, just short of the line, at the moment of the start. There are innumerable ways to try to get your boat to this position and very often the best laid plans cannot be carried out because of all the variables one may encounter. Without some sense of one's rights, the chances for an effective start are diminished.

Theoretically, the perfect starting line for a windward start is at a right angle to the wind direction. I say theoretically, because the wind is almost never that steady. Many times the line is at a right angle to the average wind direction. The committee boat will almost always be placed on the starboard end of the line as you face the first mark from the start and the port

The Olympic and modified Olympic courses. There is actually one less windward leg to a modified Olympic.

71

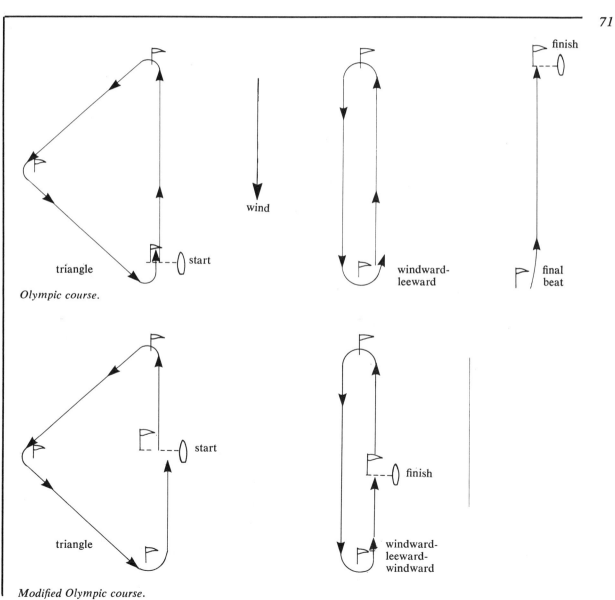

wind

triangle

start

Olympic course.

windward-leeward

finish

final beat

triangle

start

finish

windward-leeward-windward

Modified Olympic course.

Shortly after a start at the 1979 Worlds in Medemblik, Holland. Beyond the shoreline dyke, the land stretches off for miles, below sea level. No. 132 seems to be in good shape, unless 133 to leeward can squeeze up and dose him with backwind. No. 139 checks over his shoulders to see if there's room to tack out of there; if the right side of the course is favored he may be the first one over there and recoup a mediocre start. No. 147 is thoroughly blanketed and has just hit a wave; he'd be smart to tack and take the stern of 112 just to clear his air. Note the midline sag.

(Top) *The leeward end is slightly favored at the start of this race of the Inter-Class Solo Championships. Note that three boats were late (5, 8, and hidden) trying to find a hole. The three that opted not to fight it out down there seem to be doing all right, especially No. 1. It's better to get a fast start in clear air than to be at the favored end and buried.*

(Bottom) *A typical shifty-wind start. Some skippers think the windward* end is favored, others are driving for the leeward end, and the boats in the middle have sagged off the line. The North Americans, Indian Lake, Ohio, 1975. Will White won the pin end (31582).*

At the National Team Race Championships in 1974, Rip Fisher (20129) manages a dangerous port-tack start in light air. He was able to tack in time and get a safe leeward position on two competitors. I know, because I took the picture.

74

(Top) *A typical jam-up at the leeward end of the starting line— Aruba Worlds, 1974. Numbers 544, 549 and 542 are too early, but managed to peel off in time.*

(Center) *577, trying to stall before the gun, loses steerage and hangs up on the leeward pin.*

(Bottom) *On the other hand, 599 has cleared a nice hole to leeward, and may have the best start of all, unless 620 clears the pin with a full head of steam.*

end will have a buoy or marker. Since almost all boats will start on starboard tack—the right-of-way tack—the port end has come to be known as the leeward end and the starboard end has become known as the windward end.

One thing that the new competitor may not realize is that any point on the line is the same sailing distance from the windward mark as any other, as long as the line is square to the wind. Most experienced sailors will try to determine which end of the line is favored. If an end is slightly favored many will congregate there and you may find yourself with the middle of the line to yourself. This could be an advantage if the line is almost square and the boats gathered at the end slow each other down.

The classic starting method, used for years by most racing sailors, was to sail away from that point on the line you wish to cross on the start, on a port-tack broad reach at a 45-degree angle from the line. If you crossed the line heading downwind at exactly one minute before the start, you would head up and tack on to starboard, close-hauled, starting about 35 seconds before the start. If the 180-degree-turning maneuver took you 10 seconds, you would then be sailing close-hauled back to the point on the line from which you started, and cross the line right on the gun. Obviously, this method takes very accurate timing. It also assumes that the boat travels the same speed on a broad reach as it does close-hauled. Most boats don't, so you have to factor in the speed differences on the two points of sailing.

Nowadays, most Sunfish sailors use what is known as the dinghy start. Like so many "modern" innovations, its invention is credited to Paul Elvström of Denmark. Under this system, the boats hover just below the line, with the sails drawing just enough to give them steerage, and try to maneuver so that they have a clear space to leeward five to three seconds before the start. At about three seconds, you sheet in, get the boat moving and cross the line with the gun.

With this system, the timing is not so exquisite, but the maneuvering is intense, since you really have to get that clear space to leeward without fouling anybody. The idea is to try to get the boats to leeward to sail a little faster than they need to, so that you can then slow up for those last few seconds before you sheet in, leaving a gap between you and the leeward boat.

If you are just starting out racing, you should probably plan to start somewhere in the middle of the line, until you have the timing down pat. Get up close to the line within the last 30 seconds of the countdown and try to keep your air clear. If a boat tries to ride over you to windward, let him do so as long as you will have clean air for about 10 seconds before the start. However, if there are only a few seconds to go before the start, pick up speed and luff him up right to the line.

If he still manages to get ahead of you, try to bear off and pick up speed, sailing straight down the line until the gun and then head up to close-hauled. If you have timed it right, you will not be over early and you will be moving in clear air. Depending on how long a line the committee has allowed for the size of the fleet, you may find this a little risky, even in the middle of the

(Top) *Why the starting line is set square to the wind. In both courses, ABC is the same distance as DEC.*

(Bottom left) *Classic timed start has been used for years, but takes very accurate timing.*

(Bottom right) *The dingy start; try to maneuver so you have a hole to leeward three to five seconds before the start.*

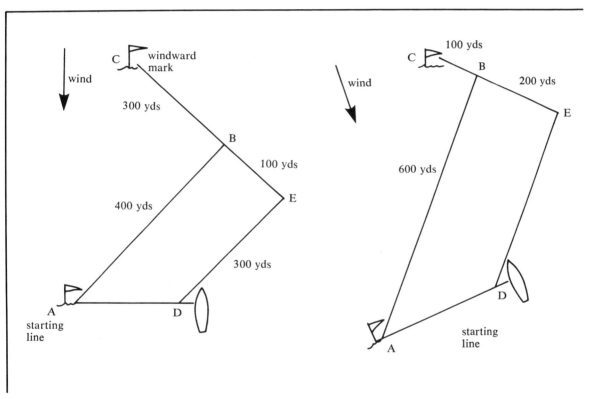

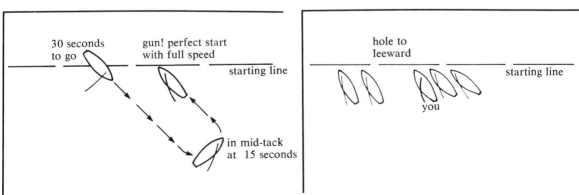

line, but it is duck soup compared to the favored end. There, the boats are really jockeying for position and many of them are getting buried.

However, sooner or later you will get good enough at starting in the middle of the line that you can start to try your hand at the favored end. Just make sure it is the favored end and not an illusion.

A good approach to the windward end start is to come up on port, tack just under the pack and then bear off the line a little with a full head of steam. If you hit the line right on the gun, you will be backwinding the rest of the fleet. If you can sail higher than most of them, they will eventually have to tack away from you.

When the leeward end of the line is favored, one way to approach the start is to sail down the line, trying to stay ahead of the fleet. As long as the fleet is overtaking you to windward, you can luff up to the line, slowing the whole parade down, until you feel it is safe to sheet in and head for the pin. If your timing is absolutely correct, you will hit the leeward end of the line right at the gun and have the whole fleet in your backwind.

To get the position at the head of the parade, it is often best to come in on port tack, flip over to starboard in front of the fleet a few dozen boat lengths from the port end of the line, and then lead the parade. However, if two or three other boats have done that ahead of you, only one of you can be right. Often, the boats will start stacking up at the leeward end several seconds before the gun and hover there before they hit the line. Even if they do manage to stall this way, they have lost their headway and the boats behind can often steam right over them. So whichever way you approach it, leading the parade is chanceful at best.

In large fleets there must be a long starting line. The committee should make the line long enough so that every boat in the fleet can have a position right on the line rather than getting itself buried in a second or third tier. Even with the longest line in the world enough boats will try for the favored end that the middle of the line is almost never cluttered. That gives you an opportunity to take advantage of midline sag, a phenomenon that almost always takes place on long starting lines. Boats sailing two or three boat lengths below the line, planning to get up on the line shortly before starting, will almost always play it safe and misjudge where the line is towards the middle. They should be cautious because being over early means either having to struggle back to the starting line and restart after the gun, if you hear the hail that you are over, or it means disqualification if you don't hear the hail and don't go back.

However, if you start at the committee boat end and sail down the line straight toward the leeward pin, you can judge your position with greater accuracy. You can sail along on a beam reach until you hear the gun, then you can harden up and go full tilt. Meanwhile, the others who have decided to start in the middle but have approached it from below the line will see you coming and be certain that you are over to windward. Nine times out of 10 they will all be a full length or more downwind of you and you will have the starting line all to your-

Typical midline sag at the start of a world championship race, Holland, 1979. No. 123 seems to be in good shape, but from the angle at which all the boats are sailing, it would seem the leeward end is quite favored.

self! In a big regatta, with 60 boats or more, this is probably the best start to make, unless one end or the other is drastically favored.

A word of caution—if the current is sweeping you towards the windward mark, you may easily be swept over early. Under these conditions half the fleet may misjudge and you will get midline bulge instead of midline sag. Then you're better off at an end rather than the middle, especially since there will probably be at least one general recall.

Sunfish races are not always started to windward. Some clubs traditionally have a fixed starting line, usually off the clubhouse dock, so that non-racing members can watch the starts and finishes. This means that as often as not, the start will be a reach or a run. There have been major Sunfish championships run under such conditions and I do not like them.

A reaching start is feeding time at the zoo. Obviously, the windward end is hopelessly favored, if the reach is anywhere from a beam to a broad reach. Everybody except the windward boat will be blanketed.

The alternative is just to figure out the angles the best way you can and hit that line right on the gun at the windward end before anyone else. Your odds are very bad. The thing to remember is that with a reaching start it is better to be the second or third boat in line at the windward end than to be the second or third boat to leeward. The others may be on the line at the gun, but you will be sailing a whole lot faster in clear air and should be able to pass them just 100 yards or so from the start.

Finally, there is the dead downwind start.

Here, the end of the line to start on will probably depend on which way you will round the first mark. You want to be on the inside because what is probably going to happen is that the fleet will spread out in a long line, everyone abeam of everyone else, and the inside boat at the mark will be like the inside skater of a game of crack-the-whip. Everyone else will have to "cartwheel" around him around the mark.

The downwind start is also one where being a little late across the line may be an advantage. Even if you manage to get the best start on the favored end—the one that will give you that inside crack-the-whip position—you are in trouble if there is a boat behind you. He can just blanket you and then come up and take an overlap on you so that he winds up with the inside position. For this reason, you often want to be on the favored end, but the *last* one to cross there.

There are endless ways to begin a race and no one could ever cover them all. Everyone has different preferences, as you will see in the interviews later in this book. No matter how well planned your start is, you must always be ready to change your plans quickly and deal with the unexpected. This is why you should have a good knowledge of the International Yacht Racing Union rules. They are a necessary tool for determining your options on any start. The ideas set forth here are just a beginning to get you thinking of the variety of tactics there are.

Though I have touched on reaching and downwind starts, they are rare. The majority of starts are to windward from a line that is square to the wind, so the first leg will be to windward.

Big fleet start with midline sag (2 seconds to gun). Note the boat that's barging, and the boats forced over the line early.

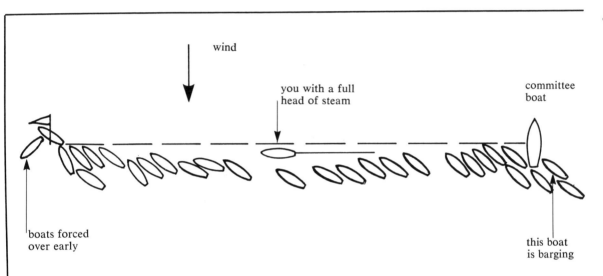

wind

you with a full head of steam

committee boat

boats forced over early

this boat is barging

Once you've made your start, you'll be concentrating on making your Sunfish go just as fast as possible. Other things being equal, the fastest way to sail is to have the sail itself working as closely as possible like a perfect airfoil. The simple rule to remember on all points of sailing is that the sail should be out as far as it will go without luffing, until it is 90 degrees off from the center line. Then you have to stop. If a sail is pulled in too far, it will stall. Stalled, a sail feels like it's pulling hard but it's really just pulling you sideways. When beating to windward, you want to test the wind continually by letting the sail get just a little soft along the luff—just a slight dimple. React to that immediately by bearing off.

Just as a bowler tries to find his groove on the alley, the sailor tries to find just the right groove going to windward. The groove will always be a little different, depending on the combination of waves and wind. But it is always there—the right combination of pinching and footing. Pinching is sailing as close to the wind as possible. Footing is cracking off from that pinched position by a few degrees, or even a fraction of a degree, to gain a little speed. I've always found that the best sailors are the ones who can snuggle up as close to the wind as possible and still keep their boats moving well.

The key to effective pinching is avoiding either a stalled sail or a stalled board. On boats like the Sunfish, with too little board or keel, one can sail so close to the wind that the board stalls and the boat starts sliding to leeward. To pinch effectively in a Sunfish, you must learn to sail on a razor's edge. Footing, although usually not so fast a way to sail, allows a greater margin for error.

There are many times when a pincher has to foot off, however. A Sunfish is not exactly designed for slicing through the waves like a 12-Meter. Its broad, flat bottom pounds; its blunt bow pushes too much water. When the waves get so big or steep and close together that your forward way is appreciably slowed, it's time to crack off a little bit, let the boom out some, and get the boat moving again.

Conditions are never the same for even one second in sailing a boat. In waves, you are either sailing uphill or down and as the waves get larger, you have to pay more and more attention to them and less and less to the direction of the wind. Usually it is best to take a rather zigzag course through the waves, trying always to go through the low spots.

It might seem logical to bear off and gain speed going up the wave and pinch up as gravity helps you down the wave. As a matter of fact, however, the opposite is usually best. In other words, you pinch up a little going uphill, and foot off and gain speed downhill. One of the reasons for this is that, as you go up the hill, you slow down, and the wind's strength is translated into greater heel and less forward movement. And heeling is one thing you don't want to do much of, especially going to windward. Moreover, you want to spend as little time on the uphill side of the wave as possible. So the best technique seems to be to get up as much speed as possible going downhill and head up going up the wave, when everything works against you.

Coming into the windward mark, most of the boats seem to have overstood—they are bearing off, compared to the two boats in the background. The sailor on the right, Mike Kerman, is mini-hiking. No. 752, Dennis Parsons, could probably bear off considerably and blanket him, squirt out ahead, and round first. If he doesn't, Mike will have an overlap. Venezuela Worlds, 1976.

That's the steering part of going to windward in waves. There are additional techniques—part of kinetic sailing—that you can use. As the boat is going down the wave, you don't have to hike as hard. The wind is translated into forward motion instead of heel. As the boat reaches the bottom of the wave, let it heel a little on purpose and hike hard as you go up the wave, resisting the heeling force, sweeping the sail a little to windward, and getting a little squirt of speed as you go over the crest of the wave. As you get to the crest, try to unweight yourself—that is, lift yourself up into the air out of the boat—putting more of the effort into your aft leg just before hitting the crest of the wave, and landing your weight back in the boat with most of it on the forward leg, giving a little push down the wave. This use of the body to steer over waves has been named "torquing." Note that this may be illegal under strict interpretation of the rules. The rationalization is that this series of exercises is really a form of steering with the body, not a way to push the boat faster.

Much Sunfish racing takes place on sheltered bodies of water, where waves have little opportunity to build up. Under such conditions, pay more attention to the wind than the water. Not only are the waves less important, but the wind is apt to be much more puffy and much more shifty. Under these conditions, most of your concentration will be on maintaining that groove —keeping the boat as close to the wind as possible while still footing.

Even in strong steady winds, the wind will change direction from time to time, and within the short space of a minute, there may be two or three barely perceptible shifts that the really sharp sailor can detect and adjust to to maintain maximum speed. I dare say many good sailors are not even conscious of doing it. If you want to get that kind of rhythm and instinct to your sailing, try keeping your eyes glued on the telltales or masthead fly.

The idea is to feather your way to windward, and it works best in light to medium air with flat water. Under those conditions, you can concentrate almost exclusively on feathering—that is, heading up with every little lift and bearing off with every little header, so you don't stall. A sailor with lesser skills will steer a straight average course, adjusting only to the gross wind shifts, and be totally baffled that another boat, seemingly steering exactly the same course, will slowly eat up to windward with better boat speed. So it's a technique worth cultivating. In its own way, this can be more exhausting than hiking out in heavy air and a steep chop, because of the constant concentration required.

As the wind picks up, a gradual change in technique is required because of increased wave action. Then, the first injunction you'll hear from practically any sailor is, "Sail it flat!" Flat doesn't mean with the mast straight up, however. Almost every good Sunfish sailor allows enough heel so that the leeward half of the bottom is horizontal—that's what's flat.

About the only exception to that is when you're coming into a really big breaking wave, and there's no way around it. In that situation, some sailors let the Sunfish heel as much as 45 degrees, letting the boat slice through the wave. If you take such a wave flat, it may

Angles of heel: when beating to windward (1) keep the boat really flat when pinching to windward in smooth water. This provides maximum lateral resistance. (2) Keep the leeward bottom flat under most other conditions when going to windward. (3) In drifting conditions, heel the boat so that the deck is nearly in the water. This keeps the sail aerodynamically effective and reduces wetted surface. (4) In light air, champion Joel Furman heels to weather. (5) Downwind, heel the boat to windward to reduce windward helm.

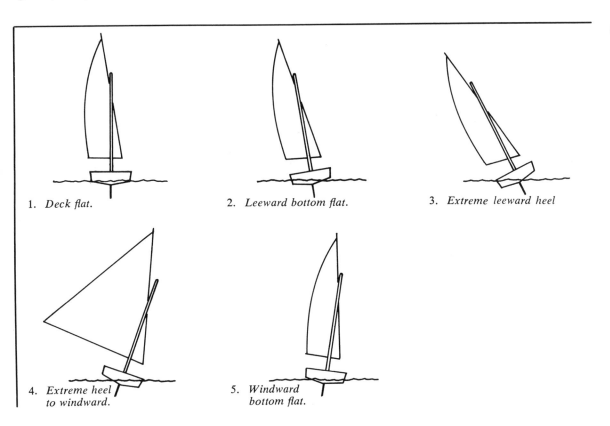

1. *Deck flat.*

2. *Leeward bottom flat.*

3. *Extreme leeward heel*

4. *Extreme heel to windward.*

5. *Windward bottom flat.*

(Top) *Big swells on the way to the windward mark, Venezuela Worlds, 1976. If 780 is on the lay line, 772 will probably be able to tack right under him with a safe leeward position, squeeze up, and round just ahead. But 709, which is crossing in front now, will have to make two quick tacks in that bouncy water, slowing down considerably. He may have to take the sterns of 772, 780, and the boat to windward of 780. Position is very important* coming in to the windward mark in a crowd.

(Bottom) *Rounding the windward mark at the 1976 Worlds in Venezuela. Eventual winner Paul Fendler is out front. No. 729 has just barely cleared the mark, but already his board is up and his sail out. However, he's on the uphill side of the wave, and Paul is pointing to a low spot, going downhill. So he's probably going a lot faster, and can* take his time getting the board up. First things first.

86

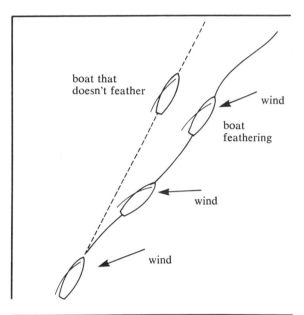

(Top) Feathering your way to windward.

(Bottom) Lifts and headers.

smack the bottom at such an angle that it will stop you practically dead in the water. Whether you take that wave flat or heeled, you want to throw your body out hard, and give a tug on the tiller, just as the wave hits.

In heavy air or trade wind conditions, when only the strongest can keep the boat flat and the sail drawing full at all times, it becomes necessary to learn to spill air by an almost constant pumping of the sheet. This is quite different from pumping the sheet to enhance flow over the sail, in effect rowing the boat to windward, a technique perfected by the real kinetics experts. The problem, of course, is that practically no one can tell where one ends and the other begins. The best trade wind sailor of the mid-70s, Gerrit Zeestraten of Curaçao, used a Harken block—with the ratchet *off*, so the sail could be let out as fast as it could be brought in.

Lifts and Headers

When the wind shifts so that you can sail closer to the mark, you've sailed into a lift. A header is the opposite—it forces you away from the mark. By and large, the right thing to do is to tack whenever you're headed. But, as with everything else in sailing, there are many exceptions. On some days, finding the little puffs of wind is more important than worrying about whether they are lifts or headers. And you have to figure out if the shift is for real. In some conditions, the wind will shift in fairly predictable patterns—every 30 seconds or as much as every 30 minutes. In other situations, the wind will shift sharply for a second or two, and then

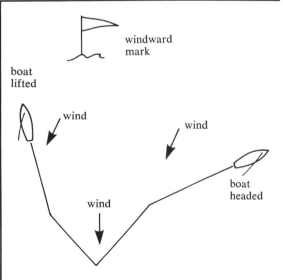

Puffs: (1) *Fan-shaped puff.* (2) *Cyclonic puff* (*northern hemisphere*) *—stronger on right.* (3) *Sheet Puffs— tack on header!*

proper
course

1. *Fan-shaped puff.*

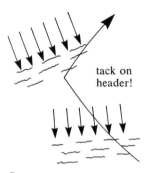

tack on
header!

proper
course

3. *Sheet puff.*

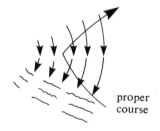

proper
course

2. *Cyclonic puff.*

slip back to its original direction or beyond. When that happens, you may tack through as much as 180 degrees, instead of 90 degrees. In other words, you have tacked into a header —a very frustrating and costly maneuver. So it pays to study the wind, and decide how long you should wait, after being headed, before tacking. Obviously, under some conditions, this will be only a second or two. In other conditions, it may be smart to wait ten seconds or so to make sure the shift is for real.

There are some generally accepted tactics to handling wind shifts, besides the obvious one of tacking on headers, and that is the obvious but often overlooked strategy of timing your tacks to stay between the rest of the fleet and the windward mark, and taking every advantage of wind shifts to cross in front of a boat with which you might have been even or even trailing.

Obviously, if everyone in the fleet is following these tactics, and is equally adept at timing the wind shifts, nobody is really going to gain an advantage. No one would gain an advantage, that is, if the shifts were the same, and at the same strength, clear across the course. But of course they never are. In really shifty and fluky winds, it is even possible to see two boats, no more than 100 yards apart, sailing in the same direction but on opposite tacks. So the advantage will go to the boats that best play the shifts in their particular areas of the course. . . or, given equal speed among the fleet, the advantage will go to those who go to the right parts of the course to pick up the best combination of shifts and wind strength.

89

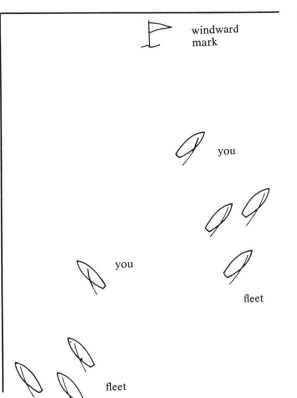

It is the ability to be where the wind shifts are best and the wind strengths are strongest that separates the really outstanding sailor from the highly competent one. It's an uncanny thing called windsense, and like any other natural ability, it can be developed through careful observation and reasoning. It is also a matter of keeping your eyes open—you can often see what the wind is doing by watching the way the other boats are sailing on the course, and, more important, by watching the action of the wind on the water. This wind action is most obvious on light, shifty days, when little cat's paws of wind make ripples on the water and are obvious for all to see. Starting with these more obvious observations, a careful watcher can learn to find wind under almost any conditions, often without even being conscious that he's doing it. This ability can reach even into the high wind conditions, when you can observe a heavier concentration of spindrift blowing off the tops of the waves in one area than in another, and avoid the too-powerful winds that can lay you flat (on the other hand, those sharp gusts of wind may flatten the waves, and actually make it easier to control the boat. There are no hard and fast rules). Occasionally, in light air, you'll see an experienced sailor stand up in the boat, scanning the water to windward for signs of wind.

Almost every top-caliber sailor will tell you to get out to the course early to figure out the wind shifts and the currents. On some courses, one side or the other will be heavily favored, either because the wind is stronger there or the current more favorable. On others, it makes most sense to work your way up the middle, tacking on the headers. And on some courses, the middle is the worst place to be—either side will do. This is often true on harbors or lakes that are roughly round, because the wind sweeps around the shores. On other courses, a point of land or tall hill will bend the wind in such a way that one side or the other is favored.

Another consideration in figuring out shifts is to decide whether the shifts are oscillating or persistent. An oscillating wind shifts back and forth on a fairly consistent basis five or 10 degrees to one side and then five or 10 degrees back. A persistently shifting wind will shift five or 10 degrees one way and not come back quite full swing. With each pair of shifts, the wind changes its average direction, moving clockwise or counterclockwise. When the wind persistently shifts towards the clockwise direction, it is called a clocking or veering wind. When it is shifting the other way, it is called a backing wind.

In a persistent shift, unless you expect the wind to lift you right up to the mark, it is better to start on the tack on which you expect to be headed. Then you can tack early, and be lifted up to the mark. If you try to take advantage of a lift initially, you will be headed on the last half of your course, and sail what is known as the great circle route. You don't want to sail the great circle route.

● **Tacking**

In tacking a Sunfish, it almost never pays to tack slowly. The boat spins on its daggerboard like the proverbial dime. Don't rely on the boat's

Handling a persistent wind shift. You should try to figure out whether the shifts are oscillating or persistent.

Clocking or veering winds, and backing winds.

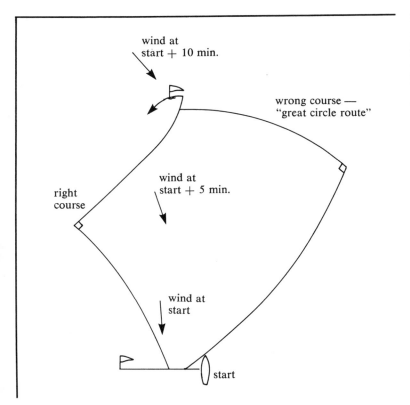

wind at start + 10 min.

wrong course — "great circle route"

wind at start + 5 min.

right course

wind at start

start

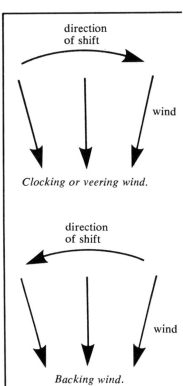

direction of shift

wind

Clocking or veering wind.

direction of shift

wind

Backing wind.

momentum to carry you through the wind, as with a heavy displacement keel boat. It will stop you dead in your tracks. It is, however, extremely important to tack in a lull between waves, or to spin it over right on the crest of a wave if you have taken it well.

Roll tacking works well with a Sunfish, but is frowned on under the new IYRU rules. Roll tacking consists of hiking hard as you come up into the eye of the wind so that the boat heels to windward, and then diving to the other side of the boat with a 180-degree pirouette, bringing it back flat as you come up on the new tack, providing a double-fanning effect of the sail that pushes you to windward an extra few feet and can give a little extra squirt of speed. It is possible to work your way to the windward mark this way in a flat calm. Constant roll tacking was frowned on even before the rules changed, although it was sometimes used to gain an inside overlap at the windward mark in light air. (But then some of the more competitive classes had developed a technique of sculling dead to windward off the starting line for several yards before falling off on a tack and sailing. "It's the only way to keep from being buried," was the reasoning. "Obviously, if everyone else is doing it, you have to do it yourself." Let's hope this kind of nonsense has died out by the time you read this.)

● Windward Tactics

Assuming you have pulled off a fairly decent start—right on the line, moving fast, with clear air—your objective is to move out with the best possible boat speed, in the direction you want to go, with a good opportunity to control the rest of the fleet. If the fleet is sizable, you will be meeting a lot of other boats, each concentrating on keeping clear air and trying to get ahead of the fleet.

It is generally advisable to stay between the bulk of the fleet and the mark and to tack when you can cross in front of a significant number of boats. Later in a regatta, when the leaders are identified, it is best to consider them as "the fleet" and ignore the also-rans, even if the also-rans are a larger clump of boats.

This general strategy holds even if you believe the leaders are heading for the wrong side of the course, depending on your reading of the odds. In other words, it is better to catch a few boats on the wrong side of the course than take a flyer on the "right" side and then get skunked when it turns out to be the wrong side after all. There will be occasions when one side of the course or the other is heavily favored. And sometimes both sides of the course are heavily favored over the center, especially on bodies of water that are roughly round in shape. In these situations, you may have to take a short hitch in the wrong direction just to free your air. But try to avoid those situations. If the lay line is heavily favored, it may be necessary to eat a little bad air to get over there, especially if you are among the leaders. It is usually better to consolidate a 10th in a large fleet than take a flyer for a first and wind up 36th.

Your strategy will also vary depending on whether you are willing to settle for the best possible place in a regatta or whether you subscribe to the philosophy that second place is no

Roll tack: (1) *Sailing flat.* (2) *Let her heel.* (3) *Hike to windward as you turn through the eye of the wind.* (4) *Bring her back up.* (5) *Hike her flat again.*

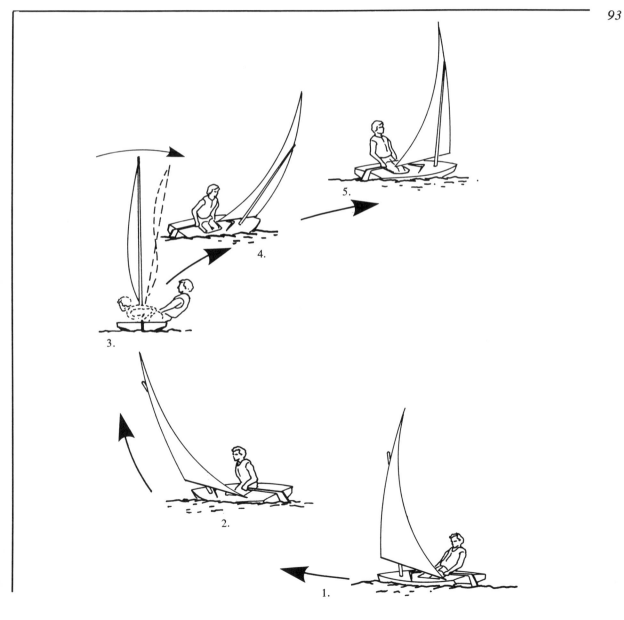

place at all and decide to go for broke and win all the marbles. In a club season championship, a string of seconds and thirds will probably do a lot more for you than an occasional brilliant first and out of the money the rest of the time.

Out on the course, when you are on starboard tack, you have the upper hand—to a point. What you don't want to happen is to have a port-tack boat tack right after crossing you, so that he is sitting on your wind—that is, his sail is stealing the wind from your sail. The next worst thing that can happen is to have a boat tack just before he crosses you in a position to stay ahead of you and backwind you— that is, the wind is thrown off his sail into the back of your sail, causing turbulence and slowing you down.

If a boat tacks on top of your wind—unless your present course is highly favored—it is probably best to tack and clear your air, tacking back as soon as you have re-established your boat speed. Failing that, you may be able to bear off as the other boat tacks, gain speed, sail through his wind shadow and clear your air. You will have lost a boat length or two to leeward, but you will have been able to maintain your course with clear air. Note that a boat to leeward and only slightly behind will still usually have clear air. To really blanket you, the other boat must be at roughly a 45-degree angle forward of your bow, right between you and the wind.

If a boat tacks on your lee bow and backwinds you, you have the choice of tacking, pinching up to get up out of his backwind, or bearing off in hopes that you can gain enough

boat speed to ride over him before he has regained full way (remember, though, that a good roll tacker will actually gain a little momentum by tacking).

When a boat tacks in your vicinity, it must stay completely out of your way while tacking. If at any point during his tack, he forces you to change course, he has committed a foul. However, the minute his sails are full, he has completed his tack, and the regular racing rules apply. If he is clear ahead or to leeward, he has the right of way. On the other hand, if he is to windward, and you gain an overlap, you have the right of way, although you have to allow ample time and opportunity for him to keep clear after you have established the overlap. You are not likely to be able to overtake a boat close to leeward, however, since he will be throwing a lot of bad air back at you.

In general, having another boat tack close to you is trouble. So your tactics, whenever possible, should encourage the other boat to stay on the other tack. A hail of "go ahead, you're clear" may do the trick, even if you have to bear off a little bit. One thing you cannot do to discourage a boat from tacking near you is to alter your course so as to confuse him, especially if you have the right of way.

Most of the time when you are racing, you really want to keep your air clear and not mess around with other boats. But towards the end of a regatta, or at the beginning, if you know that the real competition is going to be between you and one or two others, you may want to get tricky and play aggressive tactics. This really has to happen at the start, with you in a command-

Tacking to blanket and tacking to backwind. You don't want to have a port-tack boat tack right after crossing you, stealing the wind from your sail. And you don't want a boat to tack just before crossing you; that will backwind you.

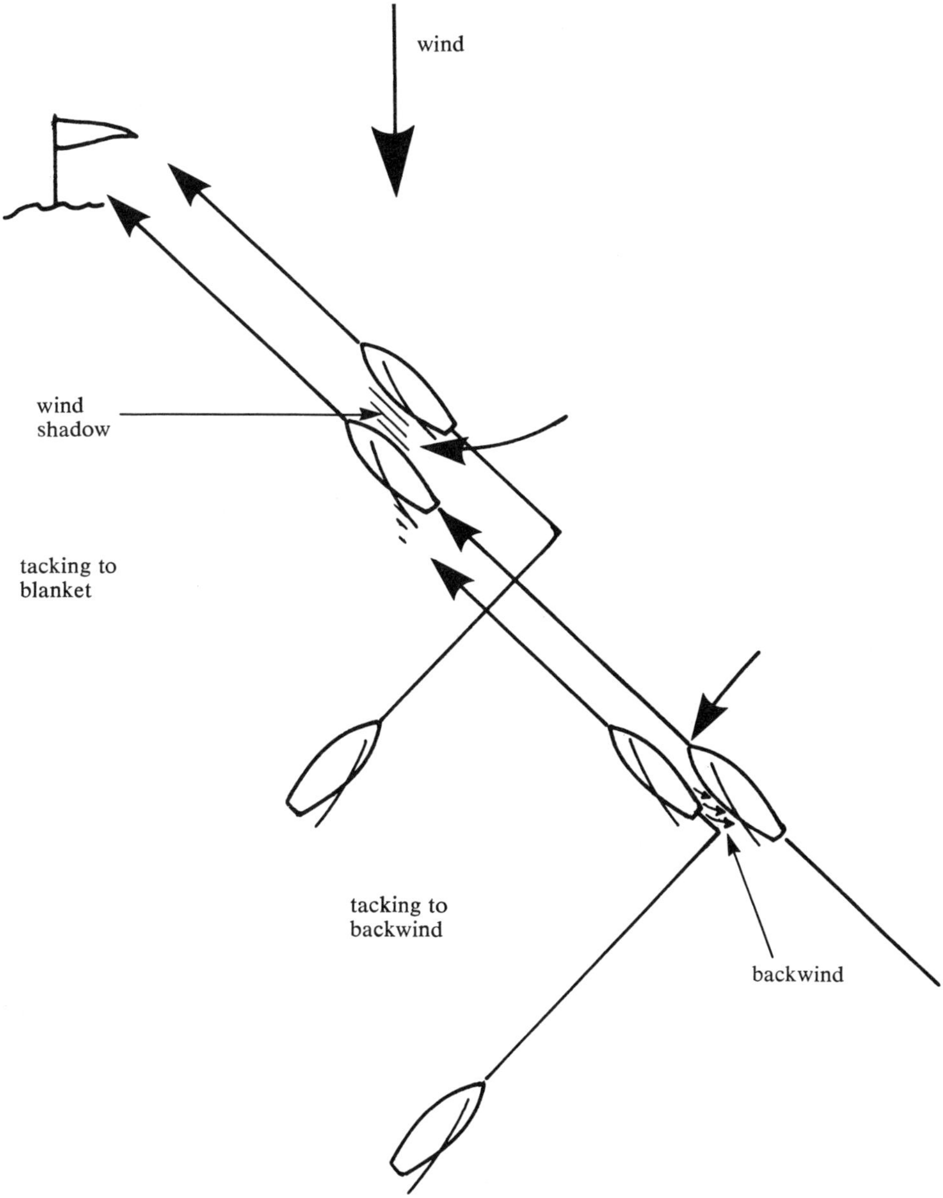

wind

wind
shadow

tacking to
blanket

tacking to
backwind

backwind

ing position over your chief competitors. But if you don't do it there, maybe you can do it somewhere out on that first windward leg during one of those crossing situations we have just discussed. In this case, you want to be able to tack on top of him and take his wind. Or maybe you want to tack just ahead of him, so that you do not have his wind, but you have him in a position where he can't get away. Or you may just tack under his lee bow and slowly squeeze up under him, slowing him down with your backwind. Sometimes you do that just to psych him out, sometimes because you want to make sure you beat him in as many races as possible.

When you do this, *most of the time* your opponent can usually just tack away. So you have to think two or three tacks ahead, to be sure you can maintain your dominant position. If you are close on his wind, and he tacks just a fraction of a second before you, he may be able to shake you off. So in the early stages of a race, it is usually better to keep a loose cover on that opponent—just making sure that you stay ahead but not disturbing his wind too much. Otherwise, you will force him into a tacking duel, and both of you will lose other boats. Remember, such aggressive tactics only make sense for a thoroughly experienced sailor working against another of equal ability or slightly greater boat speed. Since the risks of fouling the other boat are great, try such tactics only when a major championship is at stake. In the first place, it is of questionable sportsmanship, I believe—living within the letter of the law but bending the spirit. Such tactics have

seldom been used in Sunfish competition and when they have, there is usually a legacy of bad feeling. Most of us would prefer just to sail the best race we can, and may the best man win. If you would rather beat your competitor than be his friend, then by all means clamp a tight cover on him and sail him off the course. But if you sail as much for good fellowship as the thrill of victory, think twice before using the rules too aggressively.

● **The Windward Mark**

Many experienced sailors think of the windward leg as three separate parts. First, there are the few minutes after the start, when you are sorting things out, trying to get your air cleared, and trying to get to the favored side of the course. Second is the middle part of the leg, when you can concentrate on boat speed and what the wind and waves are doing, and on tacking on the headers. The last few hundred yards to the windward mark is often the most important part, when the way you approach it can mean the gain or loss of dozens of places in a tightly bunched fleet.

As with almost any other part of the course, the important thing is to be in the right position with your wind as clear as possible. The right position is usually inside—that is, closer to the mark than anybody else. Ideally, you can round the mark close aboard as you approach it on the end of the windward leg, and then make a nice smooth turn on to the reach, lined up with nobody on your wind on the starboard quarter, assuming that you are rounding the mark to port, which you always are in Olympic

competition or in Sunfish World Championships.
On the other hand, if you are on the inside as
you round on to the reach, the boat just outside you may have a little more way, or can
force you to make a tight turn and slow you
down. If he can ride over you and sit on your
wind, then the inside position isn't so hot.
Usually, however, the outside boat cannot force
you to make a sharp turn, since you have the
right of way as leeward boat after you leave
the mark.

So how do you get that inside position?
Almost always, the best way is to approach
the last few hundred yards on port tack, about
six boat lengths downwind from the mark. This
gives you a little bit of maneuvering room to find
a hole into which to tack, assuming a lot of
other boats are coming down on the starboard
lay line. Almost always, you want to avoid the
starboard lay line, because as more and more
boats join it, they have to tack farther and
farther to windward—beyond the lay line—in
order to keep their wind clear. As a result, they
sail a number of boat lengths further than they
really have to. And in a hot fleet, that can mean
the loss of several boats. However, there will
be times when the tactic of coming in on port is
just too dangerous—there are just too many
boats in that starboard lay line parade. They
may be coming all in a row, with scarcely a
boat length between them, and all aiming right
at that pin. If you tack under them, you will be
hopelessly blanketed, and you will probably
drift down below the mark, if you don't hit it.
If you are coming in from six or eight boat
lengths downwind, however, you will almost

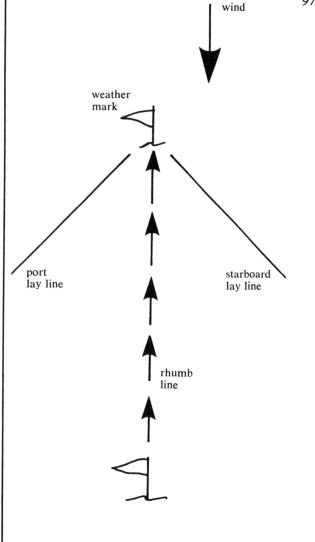

97

A good approach to the windward mark in a big fleet.

Two-boat-length circle. Overlap line is 90 degrees from center line at aftermost point (on a Sunfish's the rudder). An overlap must be gained before *lead boat* reaches *two-boat-length circle.*

98

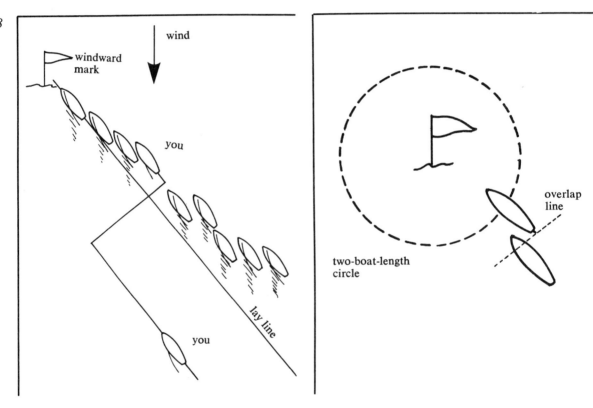

wind

windward
mark

you

lay line

you

overlap
line

two-boat-length
circle

always be able to find a hole. But your timing must be near perfect.

As with almost any other section of the course, being all alone eliminates a lot of problems. Of course, you don't want to be all alone at the tail end. The nicest place to be is all alone out in front. In small fleets, mark roundings are seldom the mass hysteria they are in a fleet of 50 or 100 boats. But at major Sunfish regattas, there will almost always be a good-sized fleet. So it is best to learn to handle yourself in a pack. Then the solo stuff will be easy.

Since more fouls probably happen at mark roundings than anywhere else, a review of some of the rules is in order. If you tack too soon and can't quite pinch up, or if the current against you is stronger than you expected and you find yourself hitting the mark, all you have to do is reround it. If you are all alone, it's easy. But if you're in a pack, remember that *all* the other boats have right of way over you until you have finished rerounding.

If you have the inside overlap going into the mark, you have the right of way. If you see that another boat is going to force you into the mark, the usual advice is to make sure that you hit the offending boat before you hit the mark. This advice is somewhat in conflict with the rule to avoid contact whenever possible, but I suppose the idea is that, if contact is unavoidable, it might as well be with the boat, before the mark. That establishes that you were forced into the mark by the offender, absolving you from the necessity to reround.

What if you are coming in on the mark on port, tack right under another boat, and force

your way in that way? The answer is that, if you can tack and fill your sails before the other boat has to alter course in any way, you can then force him up, even within the two-boat-length circle that establishes an overlap. Obviously, if you have come in from port, you have the overlap as you both enter the two-boat-length circle. The delicate part of such a maneuver is to make sure that you complete your tack before the other boat has to alter course, because the burden of proof that you did so is on you.

Rounding the windward mark outside of a boat or two is not necessarily bad. You keep your air clean and you may be able to ride over a couple of boats as you bear off on the reach, particularly if they are preoccupied with each other or aren't too aware that you are there. Then, depending on how close the boats behind you are, you have the choice of which way to head for the jibe mark. What you don't want to happen, of course, is to get caught up in somebody else's luffing match, giving the boats behind you an opportunity to sail straight for the jibe mark with clear air. That's the spot *you* want to be in. Which brings us to the next leg of the course, the reach.

7 Off the Wind

First, let's look at how to get the most boat speed on a broad reach. On an Olympic course, your second leg will be a broad reach, assuming the course has been properly laid out and the wind has not shifted. In the real world, of course, that leg can be anything from a beam reach to a run. But we will concentrate here on the most likely situation—some form of a broad reach, with the wind coming in at a 45-degree angle over the corner of your transom.

● **Reach Speed**

The first thing you want to do is let your sail out as far as it will go without luffing and then pull the board up as far as you can without inducing leeway or "crabbing." Then you want to set the heel of your boat so that it practically steers itself, which probably means heeling to windward somewhat. Your position in the cockpit will vary with the strength of the wind, but generally, short of burying the bow, you want to be quite well forward.

If the breeze is five knots or so and the water quite flat, your best bet will probably be to freeze in this position, steering as smooth and straight a course as you can. If the winds are in this speed range, but shifty and puffy, you should bear up in the lulls to maintain your speed and then bear off as the wind picks up to take you closer to the mark. Generally, we are talking about relatively small changes in course direction, between five and 10 degrees in most cases. It pays to keep your eye on the telltales and to keep the sail at the optimum angle to the wind. Whether you are sailing an arrow-straight course or playing the puffs, keep that sail just

shy of luffing or, if you are using "woollies" or telltales on the sail, concentrate on keeping them both streaming correctly, the inboard ones streaming aft, and the outboard ones occasionally taking a flick up.

As with sailing upwind, waves add a new dimension to the maximizing of boat speed. It is possible to use even little ripples to boost you along, if you can get in the right rhythm—a little pump, a little ooch, a little pull on the tiller, in sync with the waves. (Most juries, I have a hunch, will frown on this, just because it is rhythmic.) It's impossible to tell by sight when you are on the face of a ripple; it's just something you feel. I have a hunch that it's more a function of how many ripple faces and ripple backs your boat covers. Consider a fairly light day, with wavelets maybe two or three inches high, quite close together. At any one time, your boat might be sitting on two wavelet faces and one wavelet back, so that the sum of the wave forces provides a forward thrust. That's when you do your little ooch and pump. Moments later, your boat is crossing two wavelet backs and one wavelet front, and that net sum of the forces is working slightly against you. That's when you recover and get ready for the next little ooch and pump.

As the waves become larger, you will note that going downhill is considerably faster than going uphill. At a certain combination of wind strength and waves, the boat will jump up on a plane—instead of pushing through the water, it will lift up over the surface and will skip along, like a flat rock skimmed across a pond. If your boat does this before your neigh-

(Top) *At the Worlds in Venezuela, 1976, 715 has just lost a wave, but 703 has a chance to stay on if he bears off sharply. Check the other boats. Who's surfing and who's climbing?*

(Bottom) *Diane Harrison pumps hard to get her boat planing in marginal conditions at the 1976 Worlds, Venezuela. Note the lace lines progressively looser along the boom toward the clew, to free up the leech. She was probably anticipating heavy air.*

First secret of sailing fast:
(1) From close-hauled (starboard
tack) to a broad reach—keep
your sail just shy of luffing. (2)
From broad reach to running,
keep sail at 90 degrees to center
line (on either tack). (3) From close-
hauled (port tack) to a broad reach—
keep your sail just shy of luffing.
(4) You can't sail in this quadrant:
the sail luffs.

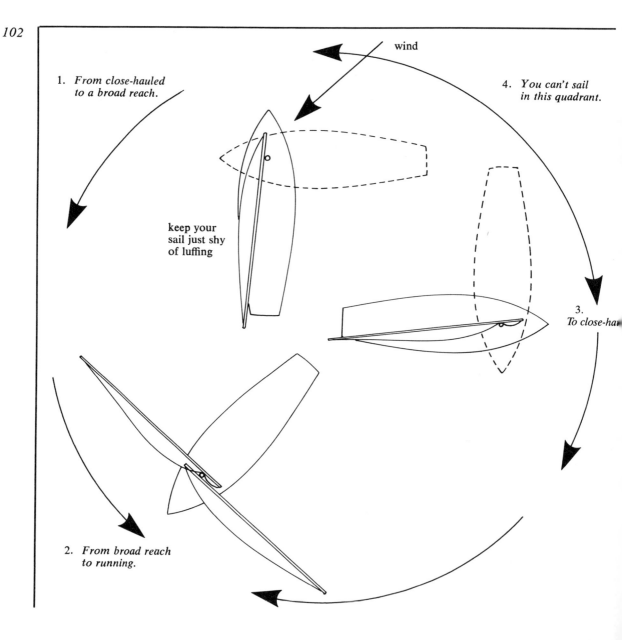

wind

1. **From close-hauled
    to a broad reach.**

4. *You can't sail
    in this quadrant.*

keep your
sail just shy
of luffing

3.
To close-ha

2. **From broad reach
    to running.**

bors', you will notice you're going maybe twice as fast as they are. In recognition of this, the USYRU rule-makers have left us one kinetic loophole. It is perfectly legal to pump the sail as many as three times going down the face of the wave, to help the boat get up on that lovely plane. It is an ability that you will have to learn if you want to be competitive in a Sunfish.

That is not to say that the only way to get on a plane and stay there is to use a lot of acrobatic sail pumping and body bouncing. Steering the right course over and through the waves can be even more important than kinetics. Most of the top downwind sailors I know are unanimous in expressing one idea: "Keep her pointing downhill" or "Head for the low spots." The technique is similar to that of a surfer's. Once he's on that comber, every fiber of his being is concentrated on staying on the forward face, making the ride last as long as possible. In point of fact, the good downwind racer wants to go one better. He wants to go down the face so fast that momentum will shoot him up over the back of another wave, so he can go down the face of the wave ahead. By being conscious of the way the waves are forming ahead, behind, and alongside, a good sailor can actually do that, if the wind is strong enough.

In steady, light-to-medium breezes, there probably won't be too much difference between your boat speed and the other boats'. In such conditions, the reaches tend to become parades, with the lighter skippers sailing a hair faster. As the wind picks up to planing conditions, the ball game changes drastically. The lighter sailors

will usually pop up on a plane sooner than the heavier ones. Since planing speed can be twice as fast as through-the-water speed, this can make for some highly frustrated heavyweights.

All is not lost, however, for the talented sailor who can pop his boat on to a plane faster than the majority of his competitors. There are a number of techniques for bringing the boat on to a plane. The most common is to give a sharp tug on the sheet—a "pump"— to provide a little extra surge of power, while giving an ooch and a scull. An ooch is a sharp body movement forward, giving a surge of momentum to the boat that breaks it free of the water and on to a plane. A scull is a tug on the tiller that provides a forward thrust against the water, like the tail of a fish. These three movements together, as the stern of the boat is lifted by a wave, can help you surf down the front of a wave for quite a while. It used to be quite legal to do so to promote surfing. Now only pumping—a maximum of three times per wave—and ooching are permitted.

This technique is not quite as effective in a Sunfish as it is in a broad flat-sterned boat like the Laser or Force 5. The tug on that wide lateen sail is not as effective as a tug on a high-aspect sail, either. However, because it is not as effective, it is harder to learn on a Sunfish, and the advantage to those who *do* learn is even greater.

In a Sunfish, many people waste time trying to make this body kinetics technique work, when they should be concentrating on sailing downhill on the waves.

Pumps and "ooches": there are a number of ways for bringing the boat on to a plane. The most common is to give a sharp tug on the sheet—a pump—to provide a little extra surge of power while also giving an ooch and a scull. A scull is a tug on the tiller that provides a forward thrust against the water, like the tail of a fish. These three movements, together, can help you surf down the front of a wave for quite a-while. It used to be legal to do all this to promote surfing. Now only pumping—a maximum of three times per wave—and ooching are permitted. Sometimes, however, the movements are over-used. Many people waste time trying to make body kinetics work when they should be concentrating on sailing downhill on the waves.

104

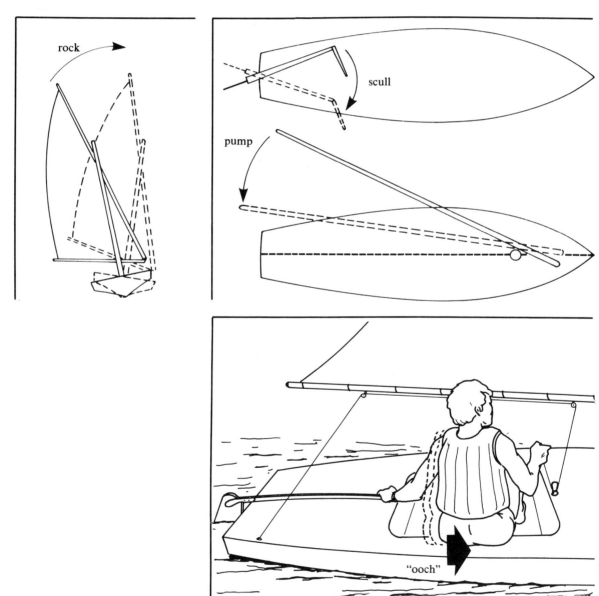

rock

scull

pump

"ooch"

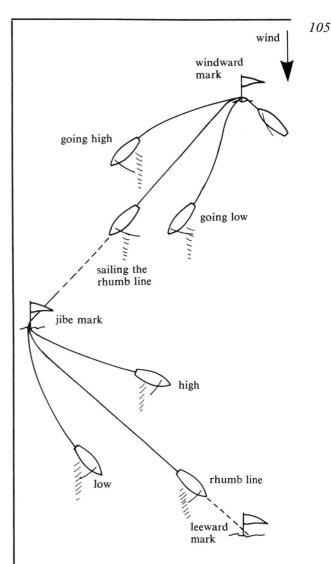

Reach Tactics

The big question on either reach is whether to go high or go low. A lot has been written about this, because there are a lot of variable factors.

One general rule—and there are a whole lot of exceptions to it—is to go low on the first reach and high on the second. The reason for this is that, going low on the first reach, you will likely be inside at the jibe mark; likewise, going high on the second reach you'll be inside at the leeward mark, permitting you to round up on to the beat to windward of anybody rounding with you.

Now the exceptions.

On rounding the weather mark, your decision may very well be made for you by your position relative to the boats immediately around you. If you have rounded inside, and there are other boats immediately on top of you, you may want to go quite high to keep your air clear. Here you are in double jeopardy. If the boat or boats behind you elect to go high with you, you may have to sail a considerable distance off-course to stay ahead and clear. Sometimes, the nearest boat may be so close that he cannot bear off without fouling you—you have the right of way, since you are the leeward boat. If you suddenly find yourself in this position, you will probably lose a lot of boats unless you come back down close to the course to the next mark. Probably the best thing to do is to bear off sharply, try to break through on the other side of your pursuer's wind shadow and hope that he'd rather sail his own race instead of chase you over the course.

On the other hand, as you round you may be able to duck down to leeward of the rhumb line to the next mark, so that you are far enough to leeward that any other boats rounding with you will not take your wind by much. That can mean from six to 20 boat lengths, depending on the wind speed and the number of boats to windward. Generally speaking, a strong, steady wind will cast the longest wind shadow. In a softer, shifty wind, the wind shadow will shift around too and be broken up, making the wind shadow less of a problem once you've gotten away from the turbulence.

The advantages of coming in on the mark from below the rest of the fleet are that you will be inside with buoy room, traveling a little faster than the rest of the fleet, which is sailing with the wind further aft. On a reach, other things being equal, the farther aft the wind is, the slower the boat goes.

Another important factor in deciding whether to go high or low on the first reaching leg is the size of the fleet, or more particularly the size of the fleet around you. If you round the windward mark with many boats close behind you, most of them will invariably go high and build a wall to windward. In that situation, the wind will be disturbed for many boat lengths to leeward, and you will lose the advantage of sailing low.

But if there are good gaps between clumps of two or three boats, you may find it advantageous to go low, because there will be clear air to leeward of those gaps. The clumps are probably battling to keep their air clear and working considerably to windward of the rhumb line. You will be sailing low by sailing the rhumb line, in which case you will get there faster and perhaps gain an advantage on several boats.

But if there are gaps between individual boats, they will likely sail only a little above the rhumb line, making it more difficult to make up the difference in distance if you sail a loop to leeward. However, if you think you are a little faster than most on the reach, it will pay off, if only to get that inside position at the mark.

All of these tactical considerations assume pretty much equal boat speed with others on that leg with you.

In planing conditions, however, especially marginal planing conditions when you can make big gains on less skillful competitors, the first priority is boat speed and keeping your air clean. Then, on the last few hundred yards of the course, try to pick your best angle on the mark to permit you to jibe cleanly around while perhaps gaining a boat or two. This could mean shooting for an inside overlap before the two-boat-length circle is reached, or rounding quite wide, letting others get tangled up with each other on the inside. In the latter situation, even though you sail a slightly longer course, you may gain because the other boats will interfere with each other. They will make the air turbulent, disturbing the pressure on the sail, and they can also throw up a lot of turbulent water.

On the second reaching leg, it is almost impossible to benefit from sailing low, especially in big fleets. Because the inside position is so critical at the leeward mark, almost everyone sails high, making that wind-stealing wall of sails even more impenetrable. Moreover, it is very difficult to come up high in the last 200 yards, slipping into the line of boats coming down on the mark to gain an overlap.

As in all sailing tactics, however, there are exceptions. It is not at all unknown for the boats in that windward parade to get so intrigued with keeping their air clear that they sail a considerable distance above the rhumb line—so much higher that when they finally fall off for the mark, they are practically running before the wind and piling up into a big mob as they take each other's wind. The boats that have gone the highest may even have to jibe twice in fairly quick succession to round the mark.

While all this is going on, you may be able to gain enough speed coming high to the mark to break through to the head of the clump that's formed and pass quite a few boats. But it is a delicate maneuver, requiring a considerable amount of finesse and luck.

Almost as good is to come up high behind such a clump of boats, take the wind of all of them as they run down on the mark and gain an inside overlap. This is an even more difficult maneuver, because you have to get that overlap before the boat or boats ahead of you have reached the two-boat-length circle described in the rules. If all those boats ahead of you have to do a double jibe around the mark, you may find yourself in a real pile-up, and it may be a lengthy protest session when you get back to shore.

It's all very exciting, but most of the time you will be better off sailing a more conservative

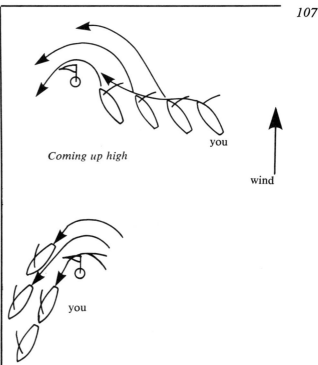

Coming up high

wind

Gaining an inside overlap.

(1)   *The leeward boat (right) is luffing up the windward boat. That's permitted, as long as the mast of the leeward boat is ahead of the helmsman of the windward one.*

(2.) *At the North Americans, Indian Lake, Ohio, 1975. Rounding the jibe mark, five boats engage in a luffing match, heading way above the rhumb line to the leeward mark. Not too bright. Will White (31582) is out ahead and above the battle. Tom Ehman (US14917) bears off*

and avoids the nonsense. Tom was runner-up; Will third.

(3)   *Dave Chapin in midjibe, with Cor van Aanholt outside. If Dave's sail hits Cor's, Dave will foul. Joel Furman is hot on their heels. Super Sunfish Champion Bill Boll (152) watches warily as he comes up closehauled to round the mark. Cor and Joel have right of way as long as they stay on starboard. Note that Cor (150) has a Jens tied on, even though the air is quite light.*

(4)   *Three of the top Americans round the jibe mark at the 1979 Worlds in Holland—Alan Scharfe (128), Don Bergman (180), and Alan Beckwith (165). Note that Alan Beckwith has grabbed his sheet directly off the boom to make it a little easier to pump. Note, too, that all the boats have Jens rigs tied on— the first Worlds where the practice was almost universal.*

(5)   *The leeward mark at the 1978 Worlds in Puerto Rico shows how far*

108

1.

3.

2.

4.

5.

the fleet can spread on the downwind leg. No. 960 has made a good rounding, if he can avoid the capsized boat. Note how 937 has rounded wide, to come up close to the mark close-hauled, a good move IF 912 didn't get an overlap before 937 got to the two-boat-length circle. If 912 got the overlap, then 937 has to give him room to round inside.

(6)   A real crowd at the jibe mark at the 1976 Worlds, Venezuela. The boats on the left are going way high of the rhumb line. No. 703 is probably smart to head low to free his air, but there are so many boats close behind him that it may not work.

(7)   Boats seem to leap out of the water at the jibe mark—Venezuela Worlds, 1976. If there's a nice gap behind these boats, the boat outside on the turn isn't hurting. If he can sail with the others, he might consider sailing across their sterns near the leeward mark, which would increase his speed, and try to get an overlap on the windward boat. With room at the mark, he'd be out ahead on the next leg, a beat.

6.

7.

Rounding the leeward mark. (1)
Close to mark at middle of round-
ing (best when you're alone).
(2) Close to mark at end of round-
ing (best in a crowd). (3) Close to
mark at start of rounding (don't
do it).

110

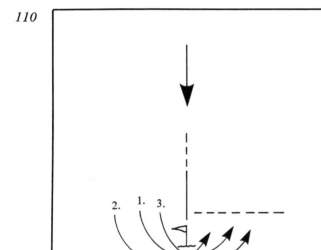

leg, either following the parade sailing high of
the rhumb line or sailing low and hoping for a
nice fat break in the line of boats that you can
sail into as you round the mark, coming up
close at the end of your rounding maneuver so
you will be as much to windward as possible
as you sheet in for the weather leg.

● **Rounding the Leeward Mark—1**
At the leeward mark, the rounding maneuver
itself can save or lose you a couple of boat
lengths, even if you are all alone. If you round
it too sharply, your rudder acts as a brake and
you actually slow down. If you come close to
the mark as you begin to round, you will complete your rounding farther away from the
mark. Other boats may round closer as they
finish rounding, pinning you to leeward so you
can't tack if you want to.

When you are several boat lengths ahead of
the next boat, make a wide rounding so that you
don't slow down, and cut the mark closest at the
bottom of the turn, leaving roughly an equal
amount of water on the downwind and upwind
sides. That way, the bottom of the loop will
take you the least distance from the windward
mark.

If there are other boats close behind, the best
way to round is a nice even turn, starting wide
and coming up close to the mark as you reach
the close-hauled position. This way, you pin
boats in your wake and have freedom to tack
if you want.

Because you end up to windward when you
make the first part of your turn wide, you can
sometimes come out ahead of a boat that has

the inside position at the mark. If you can force him to take the mark close at the start of the turn, he will either have to sweep wide, permitting you to come up inside and to windward, or he will cut the turn so tight that he slows down, giving you an opportunity to tack under his transom with better speed and so break away on starboard tack.

One tactic on approaching the leeward mark that can often gain you an inside overlap if you are behind, and that is difficult to defend against if you are ahead, is this: if you are close on another boat coming into the mark, hang back a little to starboard of the boat you are going to attack until you are about five or six boat lengths from the mark. Then swoop up sharply, sailing across your opponent's stern. You will go faster because you will be on a closer reach and you will take your opponent's air. As soon as you have an overlap, hail for room, and you have put another boat behind you. Just make sure you have completed the maneuver before your opponent reaches the two-boat-length circle.

If you are defending against this maneuver, keep a close watch on your pursuer. Occasionally take a little sharp jig up to windward, letting him know that you know what is on his mind. Make those jigs sharp and even do things to slow your boat down, so that he is forced into a position where he overlaps you to leeward. In that position, he cannot swoop up without fouling you. That forces him to go outside you around the mark.

If you can't possibly force him to leeward, at least you may be able to keep him from making

that swing to windward until you have reached the two-boat-length circle. Immediately hail, "No room"; the burden of proof if he does force his way in will be on him, and he will then be in a very tough defensive position if you protest him. Just to be on the safe side, you might swing your stern around by bearing off sharply, so that the overlap line from your stern eludes him.

If all else fails, try to swing wide so that you round just astern of him, but with the ability to cut inside him at the end of the turn, which will put you out of the worst of his bad air on the beat to windward, and at least as close to the windward mark as he is. He will be backwinding you, but that is a lot better than having him sit on your wind. Unless there are compelling strategic reasons to stay on port over to the right side of the course, you will soon be able to tack clear.

● The Second Windward Leg

If you have been able to round the leeward mark with a nice smooth circle, inside and to windward of the crowd around you, you may well have experienced the thrill of catching two or three or more boats through your astute tactical maneuver, especially if you have managed it without hitting a boat or a mark. Now you have to settle down and race that second windward leg. As mentioned before, we are assuming an Olympic course, with three full-length windward legs.

Many Sunfish regattas will be held on a modified Olympic course, which means that the start is in the middle of the windward leg.

If you draw such a course out on a piece of paper, you will see that there are really only two full-length windward legs, since you sailed the first half of one of those legs at the start and the last half on the final beat to the finish.

On a true Olympic course, the start is at the leeward mark, and the finish is at the windward mark. This means that the race committee must either arrange for two committee boats, or the committee boat must be moved from the leeward position to the windward position during the course of the race. It is much more satisfactory for the committee if they can leave the boat on station in the middle of the leg and avoid the sometimes frustrating necessity to up anchor, then drop it again and try to create a nice square finish or starting line.

Whether the course is Olympic or modified Olympic, the second leg will always be a full-length one, from leeward mark to windward mark. The strategic decision is whether to sail up the middle and play the shifts, or shoot for the corners because one side or the other is favored—or because both sides are favored over the middle. This decision becomes a more critical one when you are sailing a modified Olympic. In this case, that second windward leg is twice as long as the first or last one, and you therefore can sail twice as far from the competition. That makes things harder to control, and can make for major differences in the conditions from one side of the course to the other.

Of course, when there is a true Olympic course, those conditions are the same for all three windward legs.

On the second windward leg of a modified Olympic, however, you get twice as far away from the competition, if you sail all the way to the port or starboard lay line. If you round early, and try to cover the competition, the best thing to do is try to stay in the middle, until you can tell which way the competitors are going. If they split up, some going to port and some to starboard, you at least have the opportunity to gauge which side of the course seems to be favored—on which side the boats seem to be sailing faster, not only through the water, but also to windward. Which side has a favored wind slant, and is being lifted to the mark? Which seems to be in more favorable current?

By the second beat, the fleet has spread out pretty well, and will spread out even more on this leg. You can concentrate on covering the fleet, or tacking on the headers, or just concentrate on boat speed. Of course, you really have to do all three, but the priorities may change from race to race. In the early part of the race, you will be trying to get your air clear. Or, if you have managed to get a fairly good start, you will be concentrating on consolidating your position and staying in front of the majority of the fleet.

Those will probably be your priorities, unless you are convinced that one side of the course or the other is the place to be. Then, you may sacrifice those objectives to getting out on the favored part of the course. You may even be willing to take a little bad air to get there. As we have mentioned earlier, there are times when it pays to shoot the corners—sail all the way out to the lay line—and stay in good air or favorable current as much as possible. This is especially true on small lakes or roughly round harbors. In other cases, you may be racing along a straight shoreline, with more wind and less adverse current by the beach. Or there may be a channel out towards the edge of the course where the current is strong and favorable.

But usually, conditions will be roughly equal across the course, and it pays to keep your air clear and tack on the headers. By the second leg, you should be able to determine the best course, if you have kept track of which boats came out ahead on the first beat, and where they went. Of course, in unstable conditions, one side can be favored on one beat and vice versa.

On a long leg, like the middle windward leg of a modified Olympic course, it is not at all unusual to find that one side of the course is favored in the first half of the beat, then the other is favored on the second half. If you can get in phase with such shifting conditions, you can really get out ahead of the rest of the fleet, unless a lot of them are as lucky or as perspicacious as you are. On the other hand, you can get completely out of phase, and get tanked. When conditions are as variable as this there will usually be quite noticeable wind cells— puffs of wind traveling across the water—and agonizing dead spots in between.

I have read two theories on how to maximize the effect of those puffs—how to stay in them, and get the best angle to the mark. One theory says that each of those puffs is roughly fan-

shaped, so that if you are on starboard tack and you hit one along its right side (as it comes toward you) you will be headed. The trick then is to stay in the puff even though you are headed, on the theory that the extra speed from the extra wind will outweigh the longer course to the mark, and that you will get a lift anyway as you sail through the fan-shaped puff. On the other hand, if the puff reaches you and you are towards its far side, you will get a lift, but should tack to stay in the puff, even though it is contrary to the rule of tacking only on headers.

The second theory is that such puffs are cyclonic—that is, in the Northern Hemisphere, they tend to swirl in a clockwise direction. According to this theory, the right side of the puff as comes towards you will be stronger. If you hit a puff towards the right on starboard tack, you will get a lift, not a header. The trick under this theory is to stay on the tack until you reach the center of the cyclonic movement, and then tack again, because you will be lifted as you come out of the swirl. Under this theory you want to be on starboard tack heading into the puff and on port coming out, no matter which side you hit it on, no matter which tack you approach it on.

The actualities seem to be that both theories are somewhat correct some of the time. But most of the time, the wind just comes across in flat sheets, sometimes heading you, sometimes lifting you. Stick with the tacking-on-headers approach unless you keep finding yourself in a dead spot. Then, shift your tactics to scanning the water for puffs, and try to be

114 in them a lot more of the time than you are out of them. That can take sharp eyesight and a good sense of timing. If you are beating to windward, and see a puff straight ahead of you, by the time you reach it, it will have moved on. The trick is to gauge the speed at which you are moving, the speed at which the puff is moving, and try to lead the puff the way a skeet shooter leads the clay pigeon. It can be very discouraging, especially since puffs sometimes fade away just as you get there. But it's a very rewarding feeling when you do get in phase with the puffs, and work your way out ahead of the fleet. It is under such conditions that you will find that strange anomaly, the fastest sailor on the course finishing midfleet. He has been concentrating so much on boat speed that he has neglected to wind hunt.

Another anomaly to watch for is the occasional condition where one corner or the other of the course is so much more favored that it pays to overstand the lay line. You may have shot the corner perfectly, tacked right on the lay line, and be coming right in on the mark with free air, when you suddenly discover a boat that was behind you sailing down on you and passing you before you get to the mark. He has overstood, but found so much better air or more favorable current that it has paid off to sail the longer course. If he is a good sailor, you can assume that he figured it out. If he is a mediocre sailor, perhaps he has just lucked out. In either event, you have learned something, something that may be worth a try on the next windward leg or in the next race.

One final but very important point about the second windward leg. If it is a modified Olympic course, the regatta rules may state that you cannot pass through the starting line on your way to the windward mark. This is a precaution often instituted by the race committee to avoid possible confusion if there is more than one fleet racing, with more than one start. Consider the situation on a short course. There are four fleets—a championship series, a consolation series, juniors, and doubles. The first fleet starts just fine, but the second fleet has several general recalls. By the time the fourth fleet finally gets off, the first fleet is finishing, and the second fleet is on its second windward leg. If all three were permitted to sail through the starting line, the committee would have a terrible time tracking who is over early, who is finishing, and who is just sailing through. In almost every regatta I have attended where the finish line was off limits except for starts and finishes, someone has forgotten, sailed through, and been disqualified. Keep it in mind.

Coming in on the windward mark after the second beat, the rules are the same as for the first time around. The fleet should be more spread out, however, so things should be a little easier.

● **The Leeward or Downwind Leg**
Tactics in rounding the windward mark are much the same, whether you are heading for the jibe mark the first time around or heading for the leeward mark on the run the second time around. Here again, you want to have your air clear as you head for the leeward mark and to

The drawings below show why it can be advantageous to heel your boat to windward when sailing downwind. (1) A big lever effect, indicated by the curved arrow, is created by the sail as its center of effort moves away from the hull's center of resistance. Weather helm is the result and the tiller must be moved to counteract it, causing drag. (2) The same situation shown from astern. The turned rudder slows the boat. In (3), the boat has been heeled to windward. Now the center of effort is over the center of resistance and the rudder can be centered, reducing drag. The lever effect has been eliminated.

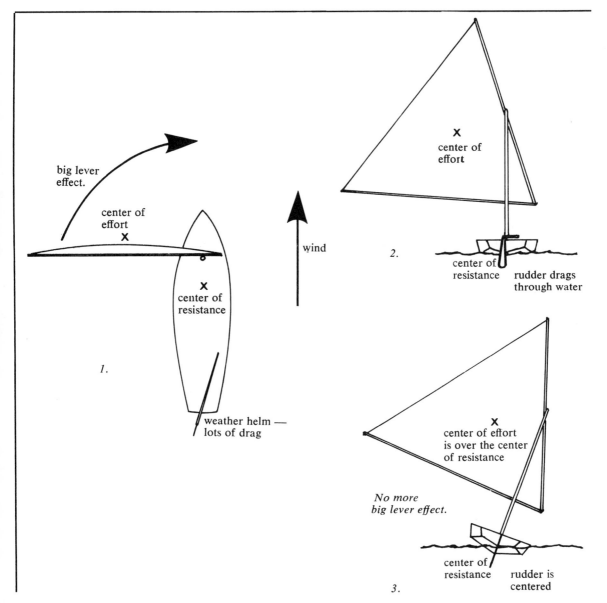

big lever effect.

center of effort
X

X
center of resistance

wind

1.

weather helm — lots of drag

X
center of effort

2.

center of resistance   rudder drags through water

X
center of effort is over the center of resistance

No more big lever effect.

center of resistance   rudder is centered

3.

be on the correct side of the course, if there is one.

Keeping your air clear as you round for the run is a little simpler than rounding onto a reach. You can sail off to the left or right a considerable distance on either tack to avoid being blanketed. On the other hand, there is often a new complication—the boats that are still beating up to the windward mark, through which you have to sail. If the course is dead downwind, it makes sense to be on starboard tack so that you don't have to worry about port-tack boats.

Just remember, you have to worry about the starboard tack boats still beating, since they will be to leeward when they are close-hauled and have right of way over you. And even the port-tack boats may be more intent on their sails and on the other boats beating with them than they are on the boats that are running free. The problem is that, in a Sunfish properly rigged for racing, the boats still beating will be hard for you to see. Even with a window in the sail, you will have to bob and weave quite a bit under most conditions to check for boats hidden by the sail.

On the downwind leg, it is usually best to heel the boat to windward to quite an extreme degree—so that the seat of your pants occasionally drags in the water. There are two reasons for doing this. The first is that the center of effort is kept over the center of the boat—the sail is not a huge lever trying to push the boat around to windward. Heeled to windward may seem like an unstable condition, especially in heavy winds, but it is actually more stable, once you have gotten used to it. The second rea-son for heeling the boat is that it reduces wetted surface, reducing hull drag and increasing your speed.

It is theoretically possible to steer a boat downwind without the rudder if your balance is good. Heel the boat hard with the sail over on top of you, and the boat will turn to leeward. Let the boat flatten out, and it will head up. Theoretically, you would then be able to pull both the rudder and the daggerboard out of the water, further reducing hull drag through the water. That's the theory; I've never seen any-body put it in practice for any length of time. The next best thing is to steer with your body as much as possible, keeping the rudder straight so it doesn't drag through the water.

There is a theory that it pays to jibe on the headers, just as it pays to tack on the headers going to windward. The idea is to try to stay on a broad reach rather than a dead run, which is supposed to improve your speed enough to make sailing the longer course worthwhile. In practice in a Sunfish, it seldom works. If you jibe downwind to hunt for puffs and find them, you may come out ahead. And in very light air, a well-executed roll jibe may actually squirt you ahead a little bit, but if you do it for only that reason, you are cheating. By and large, in a Sunfish it's best to sail a straight course as long as you can keep your air clear, assuming that wind and current conditions are fairly even across the course.

Figuring out where the wind and the current conditions are best downwind is pretty much the same as figuring them out upwind. You look for the wind's effect on the water, on sails and flags,

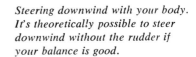

Steering downwind with your body. It's theoretically possible to steer downwind without the rudder if your balance is good.

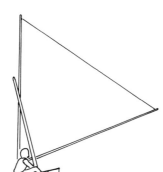

Going straight.

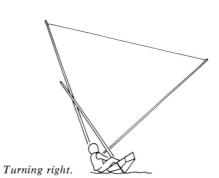

Turning right.

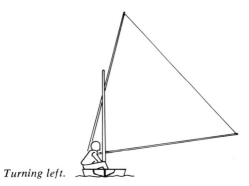

Turning left.

Death roll: Upper part of sail pulls to windward; lower part of sail pulls forward.

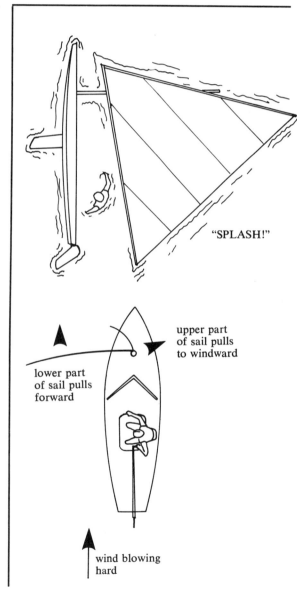

"SPLASH!"

upper part
of sail pulls
to windward

lower part
of sail pulls
forward

wind blowing
hard

on smoke. You look for current action on buoys, lobster pots, moored boats, marks of the course. Most of all, check out the other boats on the course. See which ones seem to be doing best. That's tough to do if you are leading, but being in the lead is a problem you can live with.

Besides heeling the boat to windward, you will want to have the daggerboard all the way out of the water. That means flush with the bottom of the hull, not all the way out sitting in the cockpit or on deck. If you take it all the way out of the well, water flushing up through the trunk tends to act as a brake.

Under all but the heaviest of conditions, you will want to have the sail out at a 90-degree angle from the boat, presenting as broad an area as possible to the wind. When you are running, the sail acts purely as a parachute and you get very little benefit from aerodynamic shape. There is a school of thought that says a full sail is better than a flat sail downwind, but I don't believe it makes a bit of difference. As a matter of fact, it might be well to have the sails pulled out on the spars as far as they will go, just to increase the area presented to the wind. Using the adjustable outhauls now permitted by class rules, however, is probably more trouble than it is worth. You might lose several boat lengths while fiddling with the outhauls.

In very heavy air, the sail may develop enough twist so that, if the boom is at a 90-degree angle to the boat, the top of the sail is twisted around so it presents an aerodynamic foil to the wind. But instead of pulling the boat forward, its effect is to pull the boat over to windward. That can

start you on a death roll—a capsize to windward. The solution is to haul the sail *in* as violently as possible while at the same time throwing your weight to leeward, a solution diametrically opposite to the sailor's instinct of letting the sail out whenever he is in trouble.

So in very heavy air, it is probably wise to pull the boom in to a 75- or 80-degree angle. In real survival conditions, you can often stay on a solid plane by sheeting in further and reducing the projected area even more. If the sail is too far out, it can start the boat oscillating or even lift the stern as a wave comes under it and pitchpole you. The bow digs in, the stern flies up, and you can be flipped forward like a pea being flipped off the blade of a knife.

The problem of burying the bow can start to plague you even in medium winds, depending on the waves. In medium air with a steep chop, the boat has a tendency to race down the face of a wave and into the one ahead of it. Since there is little freeboard on a Sunfish, it's like burying a shovel in the snow, and the boat tends to submarine. This is a very slow way to move through the water at a time when you should be skipping over the top of it. Moreover, the rudder has a way of popping out of the water as the bow digs in, and you have no control. You will usually round up to windward sharply and that delays your progress to the next mark considerably. But that's not so bad as the alternative. The bow might round off sharply to leeward, causing a flying jibe. Suddenly you are on the leeward side, and you will be lucky if you don't capsize.

So one of the first things you have to learn in sailing downwind in a Sunfish is how to keep that bow up out of the water. Be ready to move your weight aft—quickly! That will help bring the bow up. However, if you move too far aft, the boat will have a tendency to sit down in the water and drag its stern. Dragging your stern slows you down.

So watch your steering and try to find depressions in the waves ahead through which you can slip the bow. Unfortunately, the fastest planing angle down the wave may not be the safest, so you have to keep making split-second compromises between sailing fast and sailing into a wall of water. Under such conditions, don't try to be gentle with the boat. Sharp swings with the rudder are often necessary to flick the bow out of the way of a big wave ahead. You get to feeling that the waves are rushing at you, instead of the other way around, but the effect is just the same. Keep that bow clear!

In big swells in open oceans, you can use surfing techniques that will really move you out ahead of the competition. Paul Fendler and Mike Catalano were the first to develop these, and they seem to work best for such relative lightweights. From far astern at the Worlds in 1976 in Venezuela, it looked to me as if they were practically throwing the boat down the waves sideways. They would give a strong flick of the rudder as a wave came up under their stern, heel sharply to windward pulling the sail in to about a 45-degree angle, with the result that the sail became practically a parawing, seeming to lift the boat as well as pushing it forward. The technique was extremely success-

ful for both of them, but the best downwind sailors now seem to be able to get the same effect without such extreme maneuvers.

This sideslipping technique seems to work well in other classes as well. I once raced at the Apollo North Americans against such top-flight international sailors as Gary Jobson and Hans Fogh. Hans went into some detail at the regatta post-mortems on how important it was to get the centerboard completely out of the water, so that the boat could be slipped sideways through the water to get that parawing effect—or at least to get some air flow over the sail so that it would act as a wing a little bit, instead of a barn door.

Most of the top sailors agree, however, that the single most important technique to learn is to keep the boat moving downhill as much of the time as you can. Be conscious of the waves all around you. In time, you will learn what the waves behind you are doing from the action of the waves on either side and ahead. Like riding a bicycle, it is a matter of instinctive feedback from the vehicle you are riding.

Downwind, all other factors being equal, the most important rule to remember is, "Sail downhill!"

● Rounding the Leeward Mark—2

Rounding the leeward mark after the run is very similar to rounding it after the reaching legs. In fact, the last couple of hundred yards to the leeward mark are often identical with the reach, when the whole fleet will have sailed to weather of the rhumb line on the reach and the last few hundred yards are actually running down to the mark. All the options mentioned in the section on rounding the leeward mark after the reach apply here. As in that situation, the most important thing is to try to round up inside at the end of the turn, so that you are close-hauled as you pass the mark close aboard.

The Last Beat

You are now on the last beat to the finish. If it is a true Olympic course, you should have the windward leg pretty well figured out by now. But don't bet on it. Don't become complacent about it. Watch what is going on around you just as carefully as you did on the first leg, because conditions will probably have changed a bit. Has the tide changed? Has the wind shifted? Has the favored side changed?

If you are sailing in an oscillating wind, you may have rounded in the same part of the cycle the first two times, but be in the opposite phase of the cycle this time. In other words, the starboard tack may have been the lifted tack the first two times but this time the port tack is favored at the start of the leg. If there is shoreline in view ahead, try to remember what point on shore you were headed for as you rounded up close-hauled on port the first two times. If you are lifted above that point this time, you will probably want to stay on port until the wind shifts. If you are sailing below that point, you will probably want to tack on to starboard, and stay on that until you're headed. If there are no land references, try to remember the same basic data from your compass courses the first two times around.

A land reference is more accurate if there is

one, but if you really plan to sail the Sunfish circuit and compete in the major regattas on open water, you will be smart to compare those shore points with your compass reading, so that you learn to read your compass and rely on it.

If you are sailing a modified Olympic, that last windward leg will be shorter, and you will probably pay more attention to tactics than to strategy. For some reason, many sailors seem to let down on this short leg. They seem to feel that because it is short they are pretty much frozen in the position in which they rounded the last leeward mark. Not so! If most of the others are letting down, and you give it a last fierce burst of concentration, you can often pick up quite a few boats on this leg.

Because all the boats are sailing into a funnel, with the finish line at the neck, it becomes clearer and clearer which boats are favored, and which are not. If you concentrate on covering the boats behind and try to overtake the boats ahead, taking advantage of every small shift and puff, and if all the others feel they are in a parade, you have a tremendous advantage. It's like an Arnold Palmer charge at the end of a tournament. So bear down and don't let up on that last leg. Next to the first few hundred yards after the start, it is the most important part of the race.

8 *The Finish*

122 Before you get to the point where you have to commit yourself to one end of the finish line or the other, try to figure out which end of the line is closer. Finish lines are very seldom square to the wind, any more than starting lines are. However, the finish line will usually be considerably shorter, since the whole fleet doesn't have to cross at once. Nevertheless, you can lose a boat or two—or considerably more, in a tightly packed fleet—by heading for the wrong end of the line.

On a course where the finish line is set before the start of a race, or where you can pass it on the windward leg of an Olympic or modified Olympic course, remember to observe which end is closer as you pass close aboard. But remember, conditions are seldom steady, so be conscious of any change in wind direction.

● Windward Finishes

When you are beating to the finish, the important thing is to judge the finish line against the mean direction of the wind. This could mean that the end of the line that is closest to the last mark is not the closest in terms of wind direction. If the last leg to the finish is a reach or a run, however, judge the correct end by its proximity to the last mark.

Check that line repeatedly as you work your way up the last windward leg until you are fairly certain of the favored end, if there is one. Of course, if the line is square, that gives you a bit of latitude, and you can concentrate on crossing with clear air.

If you are in the lead, it makes sense to get over close to your competition, so that even if you all cross at the wrong end of the line, you will cross together and you will have saved your place. If you feel that going to what you think is the favored side of the course is more important than covering the competition, you may find that you were right—that you have sailed faster—but that your competitor nips you at the line because *he* found the favored end. If there are a number of boats ahead of you, you can usually determine the favored end by watching them finish.

Other things being equal, you will want to cross the line on starboard tack. However, there are exceptions. If the committee boat is large and parked on the starboard end of the line, you will want to avoid coming close to it on starboard, even if it is the favored end. That big committee boat can start blanketing you and slowing you down several boat lengths from the finish. However, if you do have to come in from the starboard lay line, try to sail a little high and then swoop through the committee boat's wind shadow. In other words, it may pay to overstand by a boat length or two, just to avoid sailing up to the line in that wind shadow.

If the port or leeward end of the line is favored, you may want to come in on port just to make sure you gauge distances accurately. By crossing on port, you won't lose time tacking. Or you may want to handle it as in rounding the weather mark, when it often pays to sail in on starboard two or three boat lengths downwind from the lay line, then tacking when you know you can just clear the leeward end without bearing off.

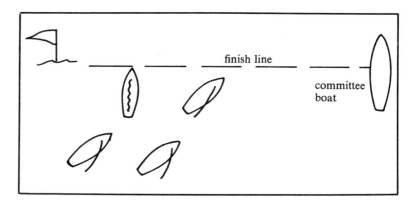

finish line

committee boat

If you have a really good view of the line, you may be able to tack half a boat length before you reach it, so that you are rounding up with full speed and can shoot your bow across the line as it crosses through the eye of the wind. If you are practically in a dead heat with another boat, you may beat him by a nose with this trick. Of course, it will only work if there are no boats close enough to prevent you from tacking.

If there is a boat on your windward quarter as you approach the line, and if it seems he is going to ride over you right at the finish, a sharp luff may poke your nose across the line just ahead of him. In fact, if he is just laying the leeward mark, you may have to luff up to clear it yourself.

On occasion, you will be crossing the finish line with a clump of other boats, and inches can make a difference. Even more important, you want to be sure that the finish-line caller on the committee boat sees you. When five or six or more boats are all crossing close together on starboard tack, the boat closest to the committee, obviously, is sure to be seen. Boats to leeward, unless they are slightly ahead of the boats to windward, will be blocked from view at the moment of crossing the line by the sails of the windward boats. So in an almost-dead-heat situation, you will probably be better off to windward.

On the other hand, in a tightly packed bunch of boats, the most leeward boat will have a safe leeward position on almost all the boats to weather, so if they sail along like this for several hundred yards, the leeward boat will probably

have worked into the lead by the time they cross the line. In these situations, the angle of the line to the wind is all-important and that should govern whether you try to be to windward or leeward. If the windward end is favored, get to that end. If the leeward end is favored—the port end—try to be the boat in the safe leeward position. You can foot off and cross before the other boats get to the line further to windward. Better yet, be all alone at the port end of the line.

Obviously, such finishes are a matter of inches. The sailor who keeps his wits about him and can take split-second advantage of what's going on for the last few boat lengths before the finish can sometimes gain two or three boats literally in the last second.

One last word. Before trying a breathtaking tactical maneuver, be sure it is worth the risk. If the maneuver is not likely to have much bearing on the final outcome of the regatta, why take the chance of being disqualified?

● **Downwind Finishes**

Not all finishes are to windward, of course. A simple triangular course or a windward/leeward course ends with the boats reaching or running across the finish line. Normally a committee will try to avoid such courses, because with the sails out parallel to the starting line, the numbers are difficult to read. However some clubs traditionally start their races off a dock so that spectators can watch starts and finishes. Or a course may be shortened for lack of wind. At any rate, you will occasionally finish on a reach or run.

123

With a triangular course, the line often stays the same as at the start, although it should be swung around to be perpendicular to the course from the jibe mark. Imagine a triangular course with marks to port. If the line is not moved, the starboard end as you reach to the finish will be heavily favored, but as a mark to be left to starboard—and you have to play it that way. Find out before the start of the race if the line is going to be moved. If it *is* going to be moved, then it may well be worth your while to head for the other end of the line, the port end. Since the distance to either mark will be the same, you will be sailing a higher, faster course by heading to the port end and you can therefore overtake some of the boats that are instinctively heading for the starboard end.

If the last leg to the finish is dead downwind, as in a windward/leeward course, the tactics are almost identical to those for the run to the leeward mark on an Olympic course. As in all the other cases, the line probably will not be square, so you want to head for the nearest end. You also have to keep your wind clear all the way down, which may mean sailing off the rhumb line.

If the starboard end of the line is favored, and all the boats are running down straight for it on starboard tack, you will be better off going to port of the lay line and then reaching up to that starboard finish-line marker at the last minute. You may be able to slip across a stern, blanket the boat, gain an overlap and slip between him and the mark. Or, if you are slightly ahead, you will get a little extra burst of speed by reaching up, then dipping down for the line at the last minute, finishing ahead even if you are blanketed for the last few feet.

Another important thing to remember about the finish is that the moment of finishing is when the first part of your boat crosses the line—normally your bow. But you haven't finished finishing until the last part of your boat clears the line. In other words, if you are going much more slowly than another boat, but your bow gets to the line ahead of his, you win the race even if your stern clears the line after his. But you are both racing and subject to the racing rules until you have cleared. So if you cross on port, and your nose crosses before a starboard boat, you have won until that point where he has to bear away to avoid hitting you—and then you have lost because you have been disqualified. Theoretically, if you have cleared before he has to change course, you have won, but I would be tempted to throw you out on the basis of poor sportsmanship. Even when you are not racing, starboard tack has the right of way.

Speaking of good sportsmanship, it is bad form to hover close to windward of the finish line after you have finished. You will be interfering with the wind of boats that are still finishing, and that's not fair. Keep sailing after you have finished until you are far enough away from the course not to interfere with others.

● **After the Race**

Some of the most valuable hours at a regatta, especially for the novice, are spent not on the course, but in discussions afterwards. The post-mortems can be invaluable. Why did the winners sail the courses they did? How did they manage to avoid the holes or stay out of the bad current? How did they know that the wind was going to shift? How did they pick their way through that steep chop? How did they manage to stay clear of that mess at the leeward mark? Why did they start in the middle of the line, even though the leeward end seemed favored? Get involved in those discussions. At first, you won't even know the questions to ask. By listening closely, you will learn a lot. And don't be shy about it. Sunfish sailors are a friendly lot and like nothing better than to discuss the strategies and tactics that helped them win or the mistakes that helped them lose.

Then, if you are really serious, go one step further. Keep a journal. For several years, when the Darien Sunfish Yacht Racing Association was breeding regatta winners by the dozens, Larry Lewis used to write a report of every Sunday's racing. He would have it mimeographed and hand out copies to the rest of the sailors the following week. He seemed to have total recall and was a keen observer. I am convinced that Larry did more to turn Bob Bowles, Bob Bushnell, Carl Knight and myself into champions of the late '60s and early '70s than we did ourselves.

The champion of champions in those days, Carl Knight, also kept his own journal. He would review it before every regatta, which not only helped him to psych himself up but also reminded him of past mistakes or techniques that worked. Of the current champions, Derrick Fries also keeps a diary.

I don't know if Paul Fendler keeps a diary.

He does have a corollary practice. He was one of the first to practice psychic sailing—going over and over again in his mind past races and imaginary races with situations he extrapolated from his memory bank. Then, when faced with a similar situation, he would react instinctively, doing the right thing more often than not before he even had a chance to think.

9 Interviews with the Champions

I once made a survey of the competitors returning on a plane to New York from the World Championships in Venezuela in 1976. I asked them if they ever sailed their Sunfish just for the fun of it, or only when they were racing. The winners, the consistent champions, got downright poetic about the pleasure they get from sailing. Many of them jump into their boats whenever they can, just to sail. They love to hang out in the hot sun when barely a zephyr is stirring. And they love to get out in gales that would blow your breath back down your throat (the kind of weather that makes race committees cancel races) just to pit themselves against the storm.

When you think about it, that's not surprising. Given two individuals of equal talent, which one is most likely to win? The one who races every chance he gets, *and* puts time in on the water just for the fun of it, or the one who only races? In terms of hours of practice alone, the one who just loves sailing is bound to come out on top more often. But I think it is more than that. I think it comes from a sense of unity with wind and water and boat. Once in love with sailing, you don't fall out of love. And that's what probably separates the true champion from the also-rans or the occasional flash-in-the-pans.

As a former editor of *Motor Boating and Sailing* said in print a few years ago, after his first sail in a Sunfish, "Nothing, but nothing, should be that good the first time; not the first beer, first dish of yogurt, first love." Following are interviews with Sunfish sailors who sail for the fun of it but who also have become champion racers.

Mike Catalano

Mike Catalano started sailing in Connecticut, dominated Sunfish fleets a couple of summers in Wisconsin and Minnesota, and now lives in Florida. The one-time "enfant terrible" of Sunfish sailing, he competed in his first Worlds at the age of 16. He has won innumerable Midwinter and Southeast Regional titles in both Sunfish and Force 5s, but the North American and World titles have managed to elude him, even though he was often clearly the fastest man on the course.

White: Let's talk about sailing upwind. What about kinetics?
Catalano: Upwind, I don't even know what I do with my body. I don't pump and rock the way a lot of people do in waves upwind. I do that a lot downwind, but upwind I think I am more conscious of heeling than I am of back-and-forth movement. If I see a puff coming, I hike out before it gets there. That works.
W: Do you use woollies on the sail?
C: No, because I feel they're very deceptive. All they do is keep you from pointing high enough. I think other kinds of telltales, out front at eye level, are important upwind. I'm always on the verge of luffing with my main and the way to do that is to use telltales that are in your line of vision, so you're constantly looking at them.
W: What is the important thing off the wind?
C: If there are waves, sail the waves. You may be way off course a lot of the time, but who cares? Don't worry about the course. Sometimes, it's good to get in the wake of another Sunfish.

That is the best tactic in the world for getting an overlap at the mark, but you have to plan it and time it right. I go for the big splashy ending at the buoy. I get seven boat lengths behind a guy with a wake and when I think it's the right time, I jump on the wake, pump down the wave and stick my bow just inside his stern before the two-boat-length circle at the mark. I've done that a million times. I think it's a great tactic, but timing when to get on the guy's wake is most important.

W: How about your outhaul? Do you play with that?

C: No, I don't have an adjustable outhaul. I believe in keeping the boat so simple, it's sickening. My boat has none of that stuff. The only time I ever adjust the outhaul is if the wind goes from real strong to real light between races. Then I drop the sail and slack off the outhauls.

W: Let's switch to the start. What's your favorite start?

C: You'll always see me in on top of the starting line. I make my decision about where I'm going to start at the last possible moment. I like to start in the middle and take advantage of midline sag. Many times people yell that I'm over the line, but I don't listen to them. I cannot remember a time when I have been early. I just keep going and then I'm free.

W: Suppose you get a bad start and you're kind of buried? What do you do?

C: You have two choices. You can sail through the fleet or around it. You have to evaluate the situation. There are times when the fleet is sailing so poorly—they're all on the wrong tack— that you can sail right through the middle of

Mike Catalano has won many Sunfish titles, though the North American and World titles have eluded him.

them on the opposite tack with better boat speed. If the fleet is sailing pretty well and there are wild wind shifts to the side, go for a corner. You could end up in the top 10 or 80th, but generally if you're a good sailor and go to the corner intelligently, you will gain. People who go into the corner blindly never win, except maybe once a year—because they get real lucky.

Going for a corner means going way over and going there in style. In other words, getting a lift to get you over there and then skipping only one shift. Let's say people are tacking back and forth on the oscillations, but are generally favoring the right side of the course because there is a persistent lift to the right. What I do is skip one set of oscillations and get away from the fleet. I keep sailing through a header until the next lift, when I get headed. By then the entire fleet is one whole tack to the left of me and all I've lost is one oscillation. It's a small price to pay to get around a whole mess of boats, if you're faster than they are. There has to be a persistent trend to the shifts and you have to know you're going to get something good over there. Then you can get right back up to the top of the fleet again and start sailing like a champ. Simple strategies work very well.

W: Let's get to the boat itself—the tuning. What do you do to your rudder and board?

C: My rudder and board are very simple. Unfortunately, Bob Johnstone completely ruined the one-design board by allowing all the shaping—which I was very much against—but I went out just like the rest of them and bought some Bondo auto body putty. My rudder is blunted and painted with epoxy. I also blunted the leading edge on my centerboard. I painted them both white because it helps show up any weeds I pick up.

W: How about the tiller and the hiking stick?

C: I don't use the universal joint on the tiller extension. After 20 years, I'm not going to change now.

W: What kind of handle do you put on the extension?

C: I don't. I found that if I used a ring, every time it broke I would end up falling in the water, hitting someone or getting buried. So now I have a big ball of tape on the end and a bunch of rings of tape down the tiller for a better grip. I grip the extension palm up because my biceps are stronger. I've been lifting weights and I'm getting to the point where I am strong enough to horse the boat any way I want to. I've been working out every day and my arms are so strong, they never get tired anymore. I'm improving my upwind sailing.

W: What kind of daggerboard retainer do you use?

C: A piece of shock cord that goes forward to the mast. Real simple. It also has a much more important job: It holds the spars on the trailer.

W: About the hull, do you worry about weight and stiffness?

C: No, the Sunfish I have now has a little bit of "oilcanning" somewhere, but that doesn't seem to bother it. It goes pretty fast. I've never weighed any of my Sunfish. All I know is if I worry about that, I can't sail well. I just don't care.

Years ago when I worked for Alcort, I

got accused of having a specially made boat. So I got rid of that boat and bought one right off the line. I had it picked up from a dealer and I carried the invoice around with me. The Sunfish I have now is just a regular old Sunfish I picked up two years ago, and it's just fine. I didn't get a chance to weigh it. My main criteria was price, not weight.

W: How about sail shape?

C: I'm still using the old sail, for two reasons. One, I have no money to buy a new one, and two, I had a chance to sail that new Fogh sail when it was designed and I didn't think it was any better. I think it has two or three points of sail when it's better, but I still sail fast with my old sail. In anything up to about three knots—I'm talking about drifters—I think the Fogh is better. From three knots to about 16 knots, when I am hiking out hard, the Ratsey is better. Above 16 knots, the Fogh is better if you use a Jens rig. I think the Fogh can also be fast off the wind, on a reach.

W: Talk about the Jens rig.

C: I'm not an expert. I've used it four times in very heavy air and liked it. It's very rough on the upper spar, but it works well.

W: Do you get out on the course early and check out the weather and the wind and the tide and all that?

C: No, I like to be the last guy out. Being a pilot, I call flight service the night before or in the morning, so I know the overall weather pattern. I like to know what the upper air masses are doing and what the wind is at 20,000 feet and all that, just to get an idea of what could happen. In Florida, we have to watch the heat, because that changes the wind. Even though I check the overall weather, all I have to do is look at the course—because in small boat sailing, the weather mark is only a mile away. You can turn around and look over your shoulder and see what the wind is going to do. Everything is so local, you don't need to be an expert.

I do check the starting line very carefully to see if the windward mark is directly to weather, on average, because the wind is always back and forth. This tells you if you are going to be on port or starboard tack a lot and keeps you from committing the ultimate sin: overstanding. One little tack at the mark, instead of sailing six miles and overstanding, is worth it.

W: Good to talk with you again, Mike.

Wet and tired after a race, Dave Chapin won the Sunfish World Championship in 1980.

Dave Chapin

Dave Chapin of Springfield, Illinois, has completely dominated the Sunfish class since 1977, at least when it comes to boat speed. Nevertheless, he was second at the North Americans in 1977 and fifth in 1978, despite five firsts in individual races. In 1978, he was second in the Worlds. It was not until the 1979 Worlds that he became a champion. He slipped to second in the Worlds in 1980, but regained the World crown in 1981. Meanwhile, he has won the U.S. single-handed title (the O'Day Cup) and the Snipe Class Nationals, North Americans and Worlds. He now sails for the University of Texas. Dave's brother Steve also does well. He finished 11th in the 1981 Sunfish North Americans.

White: How do you make a Sunfish go to windward? Do you use telltales?
Chapin: No, I don't use telltales. I feel confident about looking at the water to see what the wind is doing.
W: Do you consider yourself a pointer or a footer?
C: I don't consider myself a pointer, because if you are in phase, you should be footing to go to the next header. If you're pointing, every time the wind shifts you're going to lose. There are times when it is good to point if you can keep your speed up. One example is when you come off the starting line and want to squeeze off the boats above you. Another is if there are boats below you. You squeeze up for a while—if you don't want to tack— to get out of their bad air, and then drive over them.

W: How do you carry your bridle in light air?
C: I carry the mainsheet in the middle all the time, until it starts to pull the boat too far sideways. Then I let it go to both sides.
W: How about the new sail versus the old?
C: I like the new sail better, I guess. It seems fuller.
W: Do you have any problem with it puckering along the luff in light air?
C: No, I've only used the new sail at the Worlds. But you don't want it puckering along the luff—that's for sure. You should ease up the outhauls enough to relax the sail.
W: What about tacking? How do you tack in various kinds of water?
C: If the waves are not too big, I try to tack right on top of a wave. Then I can get around before the next wave hits. I tack just as the wave is passing under me.
W: How do you handle the sheet as you go through waves?
C: If a wave really stops me, I ease the sheet out a bit to get my speed back up. I'm always working the sheet a little bit. When I slow down, I ease it out and then when I get to a smooth spot, I trim it in and point higher or just trim in, and go a little faster. I don't hold the sheet in one position—that's for sure.

In general I don't think pointing pays. You have to be aware of what boat speed you're losing. Some guy may go higher than you, but if there is no wind shift you could end up in the same relative position because you have had better boat speed. You would tack and come together. But you want to be the lower guy because if you get a header, it will hit you first.

Of course if you get a lift, you would have gone the wrong way. You have to foot to the header.

I think it's really good to get your outhauls tight going upwind in really heavy air. On a reach, it's not so good, so it's a trade-off there. If it's light, it's good to have your sail really flat. Trim in the mainsheet really hard, get it down on the corner and really whale it in. I tie a rope on for a bridle so the sheet will go from side to side. I like to be able to adjust things while I'm sailing. If I hit a lull, I pull the boom up to the center for power. If I get a big puff, I kick it back down with my foot.
W: So what you're saying is that in medium winds you keep the sheet centered on the bridle eye?
C: Yes. Until I hike out, I keep it centered. Then if it starts blowing harder, I pull really hard on the mainsheet and it flattens out the sail a lot. If it's wavy, I keep it in. If there are a lot of waves, I try to steer around them.
W: Talking about catching waves off the wind . . . how do you know when one is coming? You probably don't look back. Can you tell from the water around you?
C: Yes. I look forward at the bow of the boat. I definitely don't look back. When I see the tall part of the wave going by my bow, I know it's time to look for another hole to sail down into.
W: You just want to steer downhill all the way?
C: Yes, but you don't want to sail all the way to the bottom of a wave and stop and wait for the next one. You have to reach up a lot sooner than that to keep your speed.

W: What happens when your speed dies?
C: Just remember that when you get on a wave, you should go radically down it. You'll work your way to leeward and then when there's not much more room on the wave, you should start heading up. Your apparent wind will be such that your speed will be a lot better. This way you can keep your boat going at top speed the whole time. To catch a wave, you often have to pump. "Ooching" doesn't help that much except when sailing dead downwind in really big seas.

You can learn to steer the boat by moving your weight from side to side. When you want to go down a wave, rock the boat to weather, trim the mainsheet and steer down a little. Kind of kick the boat down the wave. When you want to head up, sit in and roll the boat back over. As the chine digs in, the boat heads up. Then you flatten it back down again. If you get a couple of rocks in, it won't hurt.

W: Do you tie a vang on?
C: Yes, I tie a vang on around the gooseneck, using the halyard end.

W: How about jibing on the downwind leg? Do you do much of that to try to get the lifts right?
C: Yes, I think it's pretty important. In Aruba, I didn't jibe on one shift and I lost the regatta. I don't think Sunfish sail by the lee as well as some people think they do. It's better to keep jibing on the shifts.

W: How about moving your weight fore and aft? Do you do much of that, or is it mostly side to side?

C: I don't "ooch" very much. I find that moving from side to side is more important. When you get on a wave, you have to go straight down it, even if that is 45 degrees off your course. The lower you get, the more you're going to be able to reach up. So if you're looking to gain, take your gains as far to leeward as you have to. Even if you get five waves in a row, just work straight to leeward and you'll be able to reach up in front of the fleet in flat water. You should go high when there are no waves in light air and low when it's windy or there are good waves to ride.

W: Do you have any tricks or secrets about keeping the bow from burying?
C: Jump back. Usually, if you jump back hard, you can pop the bow out. You have to anticipate because as soon as your bow buries, it's too late. The bow goes under when you don't get out of the wave soon enough, when you ride it all the way to the end. You stick your nose in the wave and that's it.

W: How do you like to start?
C: Well, I usually have pretty good boat speed, so I like to start conservatively. I stay away from the ends of the line, especially at the Worlds, so it's hard for people to call me back. I like to squeeze up to the guy to weather of me and then drive off into the hole. Everyone knows what he would like to do, but sometimes it's hard to execute it. When you get into a good fleet, you may find that when you make your hole, someone is going to take it.

W: If the leeward end of the line is favored—

which it seems to be most of the time—why don't you fight it out down there?

C: The only time I would consider it is if someone really good is down there and that's someone I have to beat in that race. It just depends on the series. It's risky down there. It's risky at both ends, and I stay away from them if it's going to be a long race. I prefer just to hang back and not risk everything at the start.

W: Let's talk a bit about tuning a boat. What do you do to your boat?

C: I think outhaul tension is very important. I try to go out for a spin before a race and test a few things. If the boat seems to be sliding a bit too much to leeward or seems to have plenty of power but might go a little faster, I tighten the outhauls. Then if I start going upwind and the boat stops when I hit a wave and then doesn't accelerate very fast, I ease out the outhauls. I tend to adjust the outhauls a lot. I think the sail must set right. That's the key to going fast.

W: You're the first person I've ever heard say that. That's interesting. How important do you think the rudder and board are?

C: As long as they are in fairly decent shape, I don't think they really matter. I think the sail is much more important. Moving the gooseneck back in heavy air is like night and day. Take Cor van Aanholt, for example. He's the best at going in a blow and he puts his gooseneck back behind the second grommet. We practiced in Sardinia one day when it was blowing 35 knots. We had the goosenecks way back and we were about the two fastest guys out there,

especially for our weight. This was the first time I had moved my gooseneck back that far and I found that the boat laid off and almost sailed itself. You don't have to fight it as much.

W: Do you worry about the weight and stiffness of the boat?

C: I think the weight is important and I prefer a light boat. I think they're all quite weak and I don't think stiffness matters much.

W: How about your own personal preparation? Do you have any exercises that you like to do to keep fit?

C: I just like to sail. It's good to sail a lot before you go to a regatta. I don't do sit-ups or anything like that. The first thing that happens when you get tired in a race is that you lose your wind, so it's a good idea to play basketball or do something that will keep your wind up. If you want to get used to hiking out, you should go out and sail a Laser or something comparable. They will really work you out, and then when you get into a Sunfish, it will feel like nothing. I think sailing a Laser helped me a lot. My arms may get tired sometimes, but never my legs.

W: I noticed in Medemblik, Holland, that you were sailing with bare arms. Is that just to give you more maneuverability?

C: Yes, I don't like putting anything on my arms. I think it is the worst thing you can do, because your arms get tired—especially if you don't have cleats on your boat.

W: You weren't bothered by the cold?

C: Well, I don't think about it in the middle of a race, if I'm doing well. If I'm not doing

133

well . . . I always get cold *between* races. I have to wear a lot of clothing on my torso, so I don't get really cold.

W: Do you carry weight?

C: Yes, I carry 10 pounds, 15 maybe if it's blowing hard. I wear water bottles on the shoulders—they're much safer than sweat shirts. You can get rid of them quickly. I don't know what would happen if I got hit in the head with the boom and tossed into the water with sweat shirts on. If I were dazed, I'm not sure I could get them off.

W: Thanks, Dave.

Derrick Fries

Derrick Fries of Pontiac, Michigan, won his first Worlds at Miami in 1975, in relatively light air. He had been the top finisher among the Americans the previous two years and had finished well in several North Americans. Then in 1978, he walked off with another Worlds title. This series included one heavy-air race that knocked out half the fleet. He is also the winningest skipper in AMF Alcort's Force 5 class, with both World and North American titles to his credit. He took 1981 off from major competition, but sailed a lot and experimented with tuning ideas. He's a former Intercollegiate All-American.

Will: How do you make a Sunfish go to windward?

Fries: In heavy air—because the daggerboard is so small—I feel that I am always in a continuous process of depowerizing the rig to make the boat go through waves without stalling. I start by using a vang, then I tighten the outhauls, and gradually go to Jens rigs—from small Jens to medium to a big Jens.

W: What is a big Jens?

F: A big Jens for someone my size—175 pounds and six feet, one inch tall—is about 16 inches of mast exposed. For someone 130 or 140 pounds, it should be about 20 to 25 inches of exposed mast. The gooseneck has to move forward as you use a bigger and bigger Jens, as close as 15 inches to the tack. At first I was reluctant to use the Jens, thinking I was big enough and strong enough to do without it. Chapin was the one who exploited it well and showed that it is effective.

Going back to the initial question of how I make the boat go to windward, I think what I do is try to stay fluid. I use my body a fair amount and sheet very hard. Usually, as I go through a wave, I head up into it and then head off as I go down the backside. I don't know if I do it more than other people, but I like to sail a boat in waves on a little bit of a heel so that I'm not plunging the boat through the waves. You never want to sail the Sunfish through a wave, because it is so small and light it has to go up and over. I try to knife it over the wave. I sheet in and semi-pinch, but not too much, because then the boat goes dead. I try to keep it right on edge.

W: You say you heel the boat somewhat, so that half the bottom is flat?

F: Yes. If the water is really flat, I don't heel it. But if it is really blowing on an inland lake or small body of water, so there are small waves, I'll sail the boat so that half the bottom is flat. In bigger waves, I heel it more, to slice through them better. Maybe it's only psychological, but I feel that if you sail the boat on a slight heel, less of the boat is in the water, so you have reduced the wetted surface. I feel that, as in a Hobie Cat, I'm using the chine as an extra daggerboard to reduce slippage. Pierre Siegenthaler is one who does this very well, as far as I'm concerned, in all types of conditions with great deal of heel.

W: Let's talk a little bit about kinetics. What do you do upwind, if anything?

F: There is an obvious variation in techniques between sailors, and there are a number of techniques that work. I think there is a parallel between kinetics and boat speed. The more you use kinetics, the faster you are going to go. But at some point it becomes a question of legality. I feel that I use my body for steering, as opposed to just transforming energy to shoot the boat forward. At some point as I come up a wave, I swing my upper torso forward a little bit to help punch the boat through the wave. I do that in a very subtle motion.

Kinetics is a grey area. As I see it, you can use them as much as "the market will bear." Each fleet has its own definition of what's acceptable behavior and I try to be sensitive to that. You can usually analyze this sort of thing after the first race and sometimes even before it, by talking to racers on shore.

W: What do you do with your bridle?

F: I use the rope bridle now and try to gear it just like the wire one. In light air, I actually try to keep the mainsheet centered. Then as the air increases I let the sheet slide off to port when I am on starboard tack. In medium air, I like to put a knot in the rope so the sheet doesn't slide off so far to port. As the wind picks up more, I let the sheet slide freely in both directions. It's important to let the sheet off on both tacks in heavy air, not just on starboard tack. The key thing that affects leech tension is not necessarily the bridle but the degree of poundage you apply when you pull in the sheet. That's probably more important than the actual location of the bridle, at times.

W: How about your gooseneck? Do you move it around a lot?

F: Yes, I feel this is one of the most critical adjustments on the boat. If it's a light-air day, I set the gooseneck at about 17½ inches from the tack, but I don't set it tight. For downwind and all other kinds of conditions, I slide it back to around 20 inches. I adjust the gooseneck on the water. As I round the weather mark with the gooseneck at 17½ inches, I simply go forward, stretch my long arm out, grab the gooseneck with my two forefingers, and then with my thumb and little finger I slide the boom forward through the gooseneck so the whole rig goes forward. I think this helps speed and steering downwind.

As I round the leeward mark, I slide the gooseneck back, doing the same thing in reverse. It takes me about five seconds. Once in a while it will get hung up. I try to make sure it doesn't by wrapping light duct tape around the boom and then peeling it off so it leaves a gummy residue that seems to hold the gooseneck in place.

If I am sailing in light air and the velocity of the wind increases dramatically, I adjust the gooseneck as I sail upwind. I find it easier to adjust on the port tack when the gooseneck appears to be closer to me. I may lose half a boat length in the process, but in the end I gain a lot of speed.

W: Do you adjust your foot and luff?

F: As an experiment and to prove a point to myself I never adjusted my outhauls for the whole summer of 1981. I set them loosely for around eight knots of wind, and when it blew harder, I just left them. I was trying to prove that those kinds of things aren't that important and that sailing wind shifts is much more important. My boat speed seemed fine.

Generally, if I want to make adjustments, I start by adjusting the upper outhaul first. I'd say in medium air, maybe 10 to 12 knots, the upper outhaul is taut and the lower outhaul is loose. As the wind increases, I make the upper outhaul tight and the lower outhaul taut. Then as the air gets up to around 20 knots, I make both outhauls tight, probably the upper outhaul is taut and the lower outhaul is loose.

W: You talked about steering in waves, saying you head up a little as you go up the wave and then bear off and foot down as it goes past. Anything else that you do when you're steering in waves?

F: There are a couple of things that I keep aware of. I like to look ahead. When I'm sailing upwind in heavy air, I'm spending probably close to 60 to 70 percent of my time not looking at the sail but looking at the wind. I watch what's happening 300 yards ahead of me. I'm not really watching the sail; I'm sailing by feel.

When I'm sailing through waves, I'm dealing with the wave I'm on, but I'm also looking four or five waves ahead. If I see a really big wave coming and it's compact, I will attempt to steer around it. I would say I'm only successful in steering around a wave about half the time because often the wave is so large it would not be beneficial to sail around it. If it is a short stubby wave, sometimes I can plan my angle and go around it. If I can't go around a wave, I try to bear off maybe a degree, gain a bunch of speed and as I come into a big wave,

Two-time World Champion Derrick Fries of Pontiac, Michigan (1975 & 1978).

I tip the boat to leeward and slice through it. I also scoot my torso back, which propels the boat forward somewhat. I don't move very much, just a little bit.

If I find I'm constantly taking some waves over the bow even with a slight heel, I generally move farther aft. Generally, I hike out spread-eagle style, which is very comfortable for me. In heavy air and big waves, I keep my weight in about the center of the cockpit. If the waves are still a problem, then I end up sitting more toward the back of the cockpit and hiking off my aft leg, which is wedged in between the storage compartment and the top of the deck. My legs are long enough that I usually hike out off both legs. Only in the most severe conditions do I find myself scooting farther back than the center of the cockpit.

W: Can you keep it from getting mushy? I find that when I'm that far back, the wind seems to catch the bow.

F: Yes, I have the same problem, but I think having the wind catch your bow is better than having the bow submarining and taking in water over the splashboards. For the last couple of years, I've been sailing without clam cleats. I just sail with the center ratchet and never cleat the main, because it's always being trimmed and adjusted. Some people ask, "When do you rest?" I say, "If you're resting, you're not going fast."

There are many times sailing downwind when I want to slide my body weight farther forward than the clam cleats. If they're there, I have to hump over them, and it's an awkward body movement. Without the clam cleats, I can slide my buttocks very easily and help plunge the boat over the top of the wave.

W: One more thing about going to windward —telltales. You don't use the woollies on the sail?

F: I feel that telltales are extra windage and usually give you a false reading. They certainly give you a false reading on port tack, when you not only have the upper and lower spars distorting the wind, but you also have the sail against the mast and the scallops as well. I'd be very interested to watch the Sunfish sail in a wind tunnel and see how the wind actually crosses it. I would imagine it would not get flowing smoothly until the last third of the sail because there are so many things to interfere with it.

I just feel that telltales give me a false reading and I don't want to spend time looking at them. I feel I've sailed the boat long enough so I can feel if it's being trimmed optimally. I can spend more beneficial time looking at the waves and the wind coming across the water. They help me plan my strategy as I go. I feel I should be reacting to something that is about to happen, not something that has already happened. I'd rather be three or four steps ahead. Then I feel I have better insight, a psychological edge or something. I think there are many absolutely terrific sailors worldwide who use telltales successfully, but they just don't seem to fit my particular style.

W: Anything about sailing to windward in light air?

F: Yes, I think it's important to be in harmony with your boat. Your body and the boat must act together. You never want to go through any motions in steering, body adjustments or trim that are rigid or jerky, because they could disturb the flow around the boat. When a puff comes and I have to get up out of the cockpit, I sit up very slowly and stretch my legs slowly so I'm doing it in a very fluid manner. I don't ever sit up and jerk the boat down flat—I try to be graceful. That's part of my philosophy of reacting to that small board. If you jerk the boat, you will interrupt the flow around that small precious board and you will end up inhibiting your speed. Also, when I rolltack I never jerk the boat around or flap the sails—I use very fluid motion. It's all one big movement in a series of steps.

W: Let's talk about rounding the weather mark.

F: After rounding the weather mark, many people automatically start pulling up the daggerboard, adjusting the gooseneck, trying to get water out of the cockpit, untangling the main sheet, whatever. They're not concentrating and they begin losing speed. Then the guys from behind catch up.

When I round the weather mark, right away I examine the situation and get the boat moving well without making adjustments. I get myself positioned in the fleet where I want to be, high or low. Once I feel I've got my position solidified, I go ahead and raise the daggerboard, move the gooseneck, usually from about 18 inches to 20 inches, and make sure the sail is set right. Then I concentrate on speed.

Downwind in medium to heavy air. I like to put myself in the position where I'm not antagonistic. I feel that if you are going to pass someone, you should not pass right next to him. You should get far enough away from him, get in the passing lane, and go by. Many sailors, if they're going to pass someone to weather, come right up behind him and antagonize him. Then they've got a luffing match on their hands. When I'm going to pass, I get up to four or five boat lengths to weather of everybody; I get clear water and air and by the time they see me coming I'm too far to weather for them to do anything.

Many people have the philosophy that as soon as you round the weather mark you can relax a little bit and reach. That's not the case for me. I probably work harder on the reaches than I do sailing upwind. I feel I have very good control and that everything everyone else is going to do is very predictable. They're sailing from point A to point B, basically in a straight line. All I have to do is make my boat go fast and I'm going to pass people. On reaches, all I have to do is make sure I have free wind and air and then concentrate on sailing my boat right and surfing properly and I can make a lot of ground.

On the reach, I concentrate on steering with my body by heeling the boat a lot. I try to make as few rudder movements as possible. It takes energy to turn the rudder, and that has a slowing effect. I concentrate on watching the wind and water, anticipating puffs and lulls and balancing the helm so there is little rudder movement. There are situations when you have to pass someone or get up around the mark—then you have to ignore these things. But for 70 percent of the reach, that's what I try to concentrate on. In my view of a race, there is no place to rest. Even if the whole race takes an hour-and-a-half, I use 100 percent concentration.

W: You like to drop low in light air, but you go high if it picks up?

F: Yes, I think it's much more difficult to get yourself in a passing lane in light air. It's harder to get up above the fleet and actually blow by them, because the variations in speed are so much smaller. The difference between a good light-air sailor on a reach and a very good light-air sailor on a reach is not very much. It becomes more of a strategic game in light air, as opposed to a technique-type situation in heavy air. You have to evaluate each situation. If a whole series of boats is going high on a wild reach and you can get some clean waves beneath them, go for it.

Although there is so much to do as I round the weather mark, I try to anticipate where I want to be in the fleet, if I'm going to go high or low. Many times this is not possible because there's a big mess at the weather mark. It's one of those things you have to play by the moment, but if I can, I try to plan my attack way ahead of time. I also do try to do this as I come down to the leeward mark. I try to determine where I am going to tack and which side I will try to get on. Usually when you round the leeward mark, you're busy getting your boat ready. There are other boats around, and there may be people coming across on the starboard tack. There may be so much to do that many times you lose the flow. But if you have given some thought to where you want to be, you may be in a better position to handle these things.

W: Do you feel pumping works well with a Sunfish?

F: Absolutely. Pumping, as far as I'm concerned, is rhythmic sheeting of the mainsheet, which is in direct violation of the rules. But if there are five other guys who are pumping like heck and it seems to be acceptable behavior, then I'm going to pump. Pumping works very well in the Sunfish because of its surfboard-type hull.

W: What about "ooching" and sculling? . .

F: I'm not an "oocher" at all, I don't think, and I'm not a sculler. There are some incredible "oochers" in the Sunfish fleet who have made incredible breakthroughs in sailing the boat off the wind. I think one person who has done it remarkably well is Mike Catalano. He wedges his forward leg between the cockpit and the deck of the boat and flexes his thigh and pushes off the floor in every little wave. It's such a subtle motion that I don't even know if you can define it as "ooching." He's incredibly fast off the wind, and the way he does it is truly unique.

W: I've found that when a wave comes up under me, I want to get moving with a scull, an "ooch" and a pump all together. The pump is more to get the sail adjusted to the apparent wind as it moves forward. It seems to work for me. Other guys say that they don't do any of that. They just head downhill, as you were describing earlier.

F: To me, the pump is the main ingredient in getting the boat accelerating. An "ooch" may be a secondary movement and a scull I don't think I use very much.

W: How do you sail the run?

F: The Sunfish sails by the lee pretty well, so I don't worry about sailing laterally, off to one side or the other. I can concentrate on keeping the bow low and heading downhill into a trough. The Sunfish doesn't want to plane as easily downwind as it does on a reach, so you have to do a lot of steering to keep the boat going downhill as much as possible. If that makes you sail by the lee part of the time, don't worry about it. It goes just as fast that way.

I also make sure that I have a long enough mainsheet and that the sail is out all the way, 90 degrees to the center line of the boat. I heel the boat constantly to weather, even in heavy air, to balance it so I have very little rudder movement. In lighter air, with flat seas, I have the rudder almost glued to the center of the boat. If I want to head up, I flatten the boat a little bit. If I want to go to leeward, I heel the boat a little farther to windward. It's like sailing a sail board. In fact, one of the best ways to learn to increase your boat speed downwind in light air in a Sunfish is to start sailing a sail board because it teaches you how to sail a boat without a rudder.

W: How do you keep your bow from burying?

F: If I see myself coming into the backside of a wave, I automatically give a trim on the mainsheet, which has a tendency to lift the bow somewhat, and at the same time I move back in the boat. Sometimes I even try to hike back and lift the boat up with my leg, under the cockpit lip. If you can steer around a wave, fine. But it's inevitable that sometime during the downwind leg, you're going to go up the backside of a wave.

W: What is your favorite start?

F: I like to get a front-row seat and hold my station. If I can hold off the boats to weather, I will automatically develop a hole for myself to leeward. This is what I try to key on, so when I get down to four or five seconds I can sheet in, peel off a little bit, and have enough room to leeward to really jet out in front of the fleet. The Sunfish's long boom helps because if someone wants to luff you, he is going to have to go way around the boom. It also helps create your hole to leeward, if you have the boom way out. I think it's very important to be able to hold your boat on station at the starting line. But it's difficult because the boat is so light, the sail is so big and the daggerboard is so small. The boat tends to skitter around a lot. It takes a lot of practice to keep it hovering in one place. One good exercise is to have someone on shore set up an imaginary starting line and have them watch and comment on your success as you practice.

W: Do you have any tuning tips?

F: One of the things I find inherent in the Sunfish is that the bolt that goes through the tiller and head of the rudder wiggles itself loose and you end up with the cheeks of the rudder fitting loosely. I tighten this up; it's important. Also, when I buy a new boat I tip it over and make sure that the rudder brackets are aligned properly. I pretty much do this visually and if I think they're crooked, I take measurements in relation to the dagger-board and front of the boat. Another important thing I do is install inspection ports on the front vertical wall of the cockpit. I use the kind with "O" rings so there is a watertight seal and I install one on each side of the daggerboard. They provide a good view to inspect the inner hull and if I get any water inside I can pull one of these off and sponge out any water in there. This way I make sure there is absolutely no absorption in the foam or fiberglass.

When the boat comes from the factory, the splashboards are very ridged and burred. I sand them, not to reduce weight but to make sure they're smooth. A great deal of wind comes across the forward side of them and I feel that if the wind is deflected by a smooth surface it helps the speed. Also when you get water up there, if it can deflect off a smooth surface, there's less friction slowing you down. Another thing I do when I get a new boat, as well as at the beginning of every season, is take off all the fittings and bed each one in silicone to make sure it's airtight. That's very critical.

W: What kind of an end do you put on your stick?

F: I use a plastic ring but I'm thinking of going to a metal one because I've been breaking the plastic rings every once in a while and that's no fun. Obviously, I use the universal. I also try to make sure I get a tiller with an angle going up, not parallel to the deck. I mark the spars for adjustment purposes and I put a tie around the boom, under the mainsheet, so the boom doesn't get hung up on my life jacket when I tack.

One other thing I do is use several different thicknesses of mainsheet for different wind velocities. I find them very helpful. Three-eighths of an inch is the biggest I use and then I go down to one-quarter-inch line for light air. For the halyard and all the lines, I get pre-stretched line so I don't get any lag at all. Whenever I buy a new mainsheet, even the pre-stretched variety, I tie it to a tree, hook it up to my car and stretch that baby out. Then, when I put it on the boat, I get .001 percent of stretch.

W: That seems like a delicate adjustment.

F: It works well. It's amazing how much they will stretch, and you want that energy right away when you sheet in.

W: What about the shape of the edge of the board and rudder? Do you worry about them?

F: The rudder I don't worry about at all. I do pay attention to the smoothness and actual size of the daggerboard. I always sail with the old-type board and try to have the biggest size the rules will permit. I file the leading edge and make it as blunt as possible, like a semicircle. I make the trailing edge somewhat tapered, but you can't taper much because of the rules.

W: What about physical fitness?

F: I'm into that a lot; I think it's a big help. I do a combination of weights, for upper-body strengthening, and running. In the book I'm doing I talk a lot about being able to simulate sailing off the hiking bench. I don't like working on a hiking bench, but I force myself to do so.

A typical workout for me is running three miles on Tuesday, Thursday and Saturday. On Monday, Wednesday and Friday I work with weights—bench and military presses, foreleg and reverse leg curls, some isometrics on the arms, then maybe about 20 minutes of sit-ups with weights on the hiking bench. As April comes along and the lake breaks open, I sail as much as I can and on the days I sail, I don't exercise.

The areas I work on for strength are thigh muscles and muscles for hiking. Because I don't use clam cleats, I try to work a lot on forearm strength. I have to be able to hold on to the mainsheet for an hour and a half, so I do a lot of forearm curls and reverse arm curls. In about a year, I've put on a lot of weight and strength. I've been working on upper body strength, which will help in hiking and is also important for carrying weight without fatigue. The minute lactic acid builds up or the minute you have fatigue in your body, your chances of making sound, rational tactical decisions are reduced. If you could sail a fatigue-free race, your chances of thinking clearly are greatly increased. That to me is half of racing, being in shape.

W: Do you believe in getting out on the course early?

F: I definitely believe in it, but often I don't live up to my beliefs. I think it's important to get out there early to examine the starting line and the windward leg.

W: What about clothing?

F: I think it's important to dress properly. I mean not only warmly but so that your

clothing does not restrict any blood flow. Some people just wear a couple of pairs of sweat pants. On a Sunfish this may not be a good idea because when you hike out, the metal chroming on the edge will restrict the blood flow into the lower ends of your legs. If you restrict blood flow you have a bigger chance of lactic acid build-up. I wear hiking pants. They have pads in them that make it much more comfortable to hike out and keep the blood flowing.

I also think it's important, when you're doing a lot of trimming on the mainsheet and pumping off the wind, that the upper body has a lot of free movement, especially if you carry weight. That's why I like to wear sweat shirts and warm clothing. But I wear the sleeveless types so they don't restrict my movement. I don't sail with a life jacket as the last layer of clothing. It's good to wear a tee shirt or something over it because it is inevitable that when you tack with the Jens rig or whatever, the mainsheet or the boom is going to get caught on top of the life jacket as you tack. I also wear suspenders because they keep my shoulders rolled in as well as holding up my hiking shorts. Wearing the right kind of clothing is essential.

W: What do you wear on your feet?

F: I don't wear those silly boat shoes. I put on a long pair of knee socks and wear a pair of tennis shoes, hightops. I get plenty of ankle support and it seems like the rubber on the bottom of those is very good when it's wet. You get lots of traction.

You know the drainage groove off the storage area? I wedge my foot in there so when I hike out I can help pull the boat flat. When I torque my body, I flex off that leg. It's like wearing a ski boot. If your leg is wedged in there tight, whatever movement you make with your upper muscles is going to be transferred right into the ski. When I jerk my leg up, I automatically transfer my energy into the boat. I do that constantly when I'm sailing in heavy air.

W: Who do you think are the best sailors in the class?

F: Dave Chapin is absolutely a superior sailor. Remarkable. He is a very, very smart tactical sailor with a keen nose for the wind shifts. Another person who is consistently up there is Paul Odegard; I was delighted to hear he won the North Americans. Mike Catalano's good and also Paul Fendler, but Paul hasn't sailed Sunfish much lately. Cor van Aanholt is good as well.

I like the Sunfish class because it is one of the few classes that is transitional, old-to-young. The Laser class is all young people. The Sunfish class has a universal spread of people and sexes, which I think is a big benefit to the class.

W: What about women? Can they compete with the best men sailors?

F: They don't have the upper-body strength that men have. I think that when they compete against men in heavy air, they're at a disadvantage for that reason alone. In light air, I think they should be just as good. Traditionally sailing has been a man's sport, but I'd like to see many more women in it. They should be superior to men because physiologically their bodies are much more fluid. They are more flexible and agile, so in light air they should be able to excel. One who has excelled in the Laser is Suzie Pegel. She's phenomenal. I hope and I think that the number of women in sailing will continue to increase. They need to organize well and they need to get out there and do it—they cannot be shy. Women's sailing is still in the embryonic stages, and it needs a few more years before it takes off.

W: Thanks for all the tips, Derrick.

Joel Furman

Joel Furman is a light-air ace who walked away with the North American Championship in 1975 on Indian Lake in Ohio. That was mostly a series of drifters, except for one horrendous thunderstorm that scattered the fleet. He's done well in Worlds competition, winning a couple of light-air races. His dad, George, is also a perennial winner in Senior Olympic Sunfish competitions.

White: You're a demon in light air. How do you make a Sunfish go to windward in light air?
Furman: I don't know whether weight has much to do with it or not. It's kind of a compromise between pinching the boat as much as possible and keeping the windward chine in the water, heeling the boat to windward. I found this most successful when the wind is blowing between five and 10 miles per hour. I know whether it's the right time to position the boat that way from a typical coat hanger telltale. When the string is blowing about 45 degrees from vertical, that's the right time. In wind above 10 to 12 miles per hour, I sail pretty much on an even plane, like everyone else.
W: For telltales you just use a coat hanger with a piece of string sticking straight up front?
F: No, the coat hanger wire I usually use is about 14 inches long and runs in a straight plane about three feet up on the gaff, right across the front of the boat. The piece of string is about six inches long and I usually get it by pulling a canvas string out of the sail bag.

For windward work on starboard tack, if you find yourself pointing the string towards the mast, you're about right. On port tack, if you point the string toward the back edge of the sail, the leech, that's about right.

W: *And you say you actually heel to windward?*

F: Yes. I'm not sure how to describe it. When you get enough air to feel a little resistance on the tiller or the rudder, then you can heel the boat to windward. As soon as that resistance comes off the tiller, you know that the boat is no longer sliding sideways, but is going straight ahead. That's the best I can do to describe it. It seems to be very successful, especially with the lanyard system on the old sail. I found that with lace lines instead of the plastic clips, you could move the draft of the sail around.

W: *I gather that, at least in light air, you're a pincher rather than a footer?*

F: Yes, as much as possible. The idea is to get the boat footing and then pinch it up. There is kind of a break point between footing and pinching, about halfway between the two. I think most people fall off and start to foot when they feel themselves start to slide sideways. I think if you go up higher, you can go through that break point, and if you heel the boat to windward, it makes it easier. Then you lose all resistance on the tiller, so you know you're not stalled, not sideslipping. That's when you know you're going. It works. It's critical to position your weight right.

W: *What do you do when the wind picks up?*

F: The more wind there is, the farther aft I move my weight. I move to the middle of the cockpit and hike out with my legs spread in the cockpit. It feels more like working with a surfboard than a boat.

W: *What about the bridle?*

F: I let it slide on the starboard tack and I keep it in the middle on the port tack.

W: *No matter what the wind?*

F: No matter what the wind. With the new sail most people let it go on both sides. How do you do it?

W: *I really haven't learned the new sail either, but I've been tying knots so I can vary the distance it will slide. I keep it in closer in lighter air and let it go farther and farther out as the wind picks up. But I find that I'm not particularly faster that way. I like the new sail in heavy air, but I don't like it in light air.*

F: The best success I ever had with the new sail was when I bought one of the brand-new ones down in Gulfport for the North Americans. Catalano was picking on me as I was putting the new sail on the spars and because I was talking to him I made a mistake and put the sail on upside down. I didn't know I'd done it until I got out on the water and hoisted the sail. As usual I was the last one to leave the beach— I can't break precedents. I had to keep going to the starting line, which was three or four miles out. I couldn't believe how I was going by boats all the way out there. It was incredible, with the numbers upside down and the window going vertically. Before the start I had time to turn it around and I was sorry I did. I no longer had the same speed.

W: *Did you ever try it again?*

F: No, I've never done it again. I don't know if there is a variance to the draft of the sail or what, but I sure would like to try it. It probably wouldn't be legal since the Sunfish would be in the wrong position and the numbers would also be improperly positioned.

W: Mike Catalano still doesn't think the new sails are any better. He still likes his old sail.

F: Really? Well, I feel the same way as far as light air is concerned. I like my old sails. But when it gets above—actually, I'm not sure the velocity of the wind matters. I think the difference comes about when there is a chop. The newer sail definitely puts you through the chop, compared with the old sail. So that's the advantage.

W: How do you carry the foot and the luff?

F: It's hard for me to get over the old ways. I keep going back to them and that's probably why I haven't been as successful lately. I carry both the foot and luff quite tight. I don't have them as loose as everyone else usually does. Anything to keep the darts out of the sail. With my lanyard system, I'm always working to keep the darts out. I like to have a clean-looking sail. The lanyards control the leech. In light air, I tighten down on the last grommet on both the gaff and on the end of the boom. That gives the leech a bit of a curl. That curl pushes you to windward, especially if you are working in light air. It makes it easier to pinch. When it blows hard, I loosen the leech by loosening the last strings on the two grommets on the end.

W: Do you have any particular steering techniques in light air?

F: In light air I don't move the tiller at all. In fact, I try to arrange it so that the boat will sail itself without my moving the tiller for at least three to five seconds. If you can get it up to about 10 seconds, you've got it. You're steering with just your weight. That's when it's right. As little movement as possible with the tiller makes a big difference. If anything, I think I try to stay with the tiller to leeward a little bit.

W: Let's get on to reaching. What do you do?

F: I try to steer a straight course from one mark to the next. Generally, as you round the first windward mark, everyone goes to windward right away. I usually sail on a straight course for the first 15 to 25 yards and then I try to slide off to leeward as much as possible, unless it's a very close reach. If it's a medium reach, I definitely fall off to leeward as soon as possible. That way I'm clear of everyone. They think they're going like bandits, but nine times out of ten they're not sailing a true course to the next mark. Since the majority of people go to windward together, they're fighting for the same air. After you sacrifice the first 20 or 30 yards, you'll find you have clear air; unless Will White decides to contend with you. It's lonely there.

Nine times out of ten you are eliminating yourself from the typical fight at the jibe mark. When you arrive there you have the advantage of being the inside boat on the jibe and you also have the best speed toward the mark, as opposed to those who went to windward early. You can also pick your wave and go where you want to go when you are down to leeward. Coming into the mark on a collision course with the other boats, you have the right of way. You still have air coming in at the very last minute at the mark, as opposed to the boats that are dropping down. They're still fighting for air. You also have the advantage of being able to keep your boat moving.

Joel Furman, 1975 North American Champion, just after winning the last race at the 1979 Worlds in Holland.

W: How about the second reaching leg?

F: The second leg usually turns out to be a broad reach. Like everyone else, I find myself heeling the boat to windward, keeping the sail up in the air as much as possible. Again, I usually try to drop off to leeward to get away from the crowd. I find the boat actually goes faster if you're sailing below the line. For some reason, Sunfish seem to go faster when you're sailing by the lee. It gives you a better opportunity to take advantage of the waves and it gives you better boat speed.

W: What about kinetics?

F: On a reaching leg, I mentally visualize myself as being on a surfboard rather than a sailboat. You can actually gain about half a knot if you scoot forward in waves and then scoot back at the end of a series of waves. It pays to move your weight in a Sunfish. Even moving three or four inches makes a difference. The harder it blows, the less time you have to move your rear end. But just by leaning forward and back with your upper torso you can have a tremendous amount of modulation.

W: How do you keep your bow from burying?

F: I pray a lot. Sometimes it's so bad you literally have to almost hang tail off the stern of the boat.

W: You have to do a lot of steering?

F: Yes, the harder it's blowing, the more you have to steer. You can't make any mistakes. If you do, you're going to find your boat under water. Then it's all over. I think you have to do a lot with the centerboard too. Just a couple of inches of board in the water can make a big difference.

W: How about the start?

F: I like to start by myself. I think probably the bigger the regatta, the more important it is to get an excellent start. I think it's absolutely necessary to be aggressive. It's so amazing that the majority of Sunfish sailors are so intent on concentrating on their watches that they lose sight of the boats around them. You've got to be totally aware of all four directions around you and at the same time you have to computerize yourself with the time sequence. You can't be preoccupied with worrying about how much time you have left. You have to stay aware of what the situation is around you. A tremendous number of openings are going to materialize even though you see boats all around you and it seems there's nowhere for you to go. You'll find that there will be room, there will be places for you to duck into, but you must stay alert and take advantage of them to get a good start.

W: When one end of the line is favored, do you fight it out there?

F: No. Unless I'm absolutely sure that I can get the number one spot, I won't fight for it. Especially when I know that some sailors, particularly in the Sunfish league, are always there. I won't get into a fight because I have found that it's better to sacrifice proper positioning to gain that clear air spot.

W: What about weight? Do you worry about weight?

F: If it's going to blow more than 15 miles per hour, I might just as well stand on the shore and knock my knees to the wind. I feel that you have to be in about the 160- to 170-pound range to do well when it's blowing hard.

W: Have you tried wearing weight?

F: Yes, I've been wearing a water jacket for the past three years. Anytime it blows hard, I have to put it on. It helps me, and it does make a difference. I find that I'm at least within shooting or knocking distance of the front door when I get to the windward mark, as compared to when I don't wear weight. It also makes me work a lot harder to windward when I know I have the weight on me, so there's a psychological effect. It's a lot easier handling the puffs. I don't have to wear the sheet out when I get hit by them. I know I'm going to get immediate response from the boat by shifting my weight, instead of having to wait for the response after I make an alteration to the sail. The more weight you have, the better off you are. I wish my father could transfer his gut to mine.

W: How about the Jens rig? I'm sure you use it.

F: Yes. Remember the *Yacht Racing/Cruising* magazine edition from the Netherlands? I was the example of the Jens that they pictured and that really surprised me because I think I was probably the one candidate who never did really figure out how to set up that arrangement right. It never worked for me there.

I guess it was in Aruba that I finally was able to find the fine points of the rig. I learned that it is critical to keep the sail adjusted exactly right. I found that if I moved it even about half-an-inch to an inch, then I lost balance control—which made a terrific difference in my ability to go to windward. To me, the sacrifice in using the Jens was not worth it unless I needed it to survive. Even then I was sorry to use it. I think

Not all champions are men. Jean Bergman won the Women's North American Championship in 1980, and often beats the best of the men, including husband Don and all 10 of their children.

I would have done a lot better if I had not used it in the first four races in the Netherlands.

W: I didn't use it in the Netherlands and wished I had. I guess we find our excuses where we can.

F: In Aruba, it was necessary to use the Jens. My problem was that I would beat my brains out to get into about the top 15 boats to windward and then I would end up capsizing because my water jacket wouldn't clear the boom.

W: What about your board?

F: I've stayed with the original board. It still has the original shape from the factory. I use the sander and take off the varnish that they put on and then brush on fiberglass resin. I don't brush it on like everyone else does, though— with the grain. I go from one side to the other, with the water flow. Then, I sand the same way. Usually about two or three coats of that resin does the trick. I don't put any coloration in it.

W: You don't put any fiberglass on it?

F: No, the glass to me is a pain in the neck. It's going to come off if it gets hit, anyway. So what's the difference? It just adds more weight to the board.

W: Any other wrinkles or gadgets?

F: The best I've ever done was the North American Championship in Ohio. I had two watches, both of which broke after the first race. I had two compasses, both of which I lost. I didn't have anything. I had to handmake a telltale in the middle of the series because I lost the Feathermate one. That's when I started using just a regular coat hanger and the string from the sail bag.

W: Thanks, Joel.

Paul Odegard, 1981 North American Champion, takes a break at the 1976 Worlds in Venezuela.

Paul Odegard

No one has tried harder than Paul Odegard and no one ever got a bigger hand at an awards ceremony than he did when he won the 1981 Sunfish North Americans in Charleston, South Carolina, at the age of 44. It was a popular win. Paul is particularly tough upwind in heavy air and is a student of the boat. As an engineer, he applies his studies in aerodynamics and hydro-dynamics to his boat tuning. He travels every-where with a private cheering section: his lovely wife, Polly, and charming daughters, Pam and Kristin. He has also won the Northeast Regional Championship, which many feel is tougher some years than the North Americans.

White: We're just going to go around the course, first of all. Talk to me a little bit about how you make a Sunfish go to windward.
Odegard: Well, in medium to heavy air, which I really enjoy, I think one of the most important things is the hiking. A lot of sailors don't really hike properly. You should get completely over the side by hooking your feet on the main sheet as it goes through the Harken or by just barely putting a couple of toes under the cockpit lip. It makes a difference in heavy air. It's always your weight versus the boat's weight. I like to wear my weight from the waist down. Since I tend to stay wet if I'm hiking, I wear heavy sweat pants rather than weight on the shoulders. It's really tough to move around the boat with weight above the waist.

Then there's playing the waves. With the little freeboard on the bow of the Sunfish, it's very important to keep the bow up as you go through the waves. You should constantly move your body fore and aft and in and out, hiking to keep the bow from burying. You also have to really honk on the helm to keep the boat moving because there doesn't seem to be enough rudder area. I bear up as the wave approaches and then I give a good pull on the helm to get the boat to veer off down the trough. In some cases when I get a very big wave, I go almost head-to-wind and move aft, way aft, to the back of the boat, to keep the bow from being buried. I think that pinching on very big waves is even more important than trying to bear off. I've had an awful lot of success by always being a pincher rather than a footer. Even in heavy air, I try to keep the boat flat and play the waves rather than powering off.

W: But if you're pinching and you head into a wave, how do you get speed to get over it?
O: Well, you pinch and then veer off. You alternate the two.
W: Are you working the sheet too?
O: Yes, depending on how much it's blowing. As you come up the wave, sheet in; as you veer off, let the sheet out. Trouble is, in heavy air you get so damn tired.
W: How do you use the bridle?
O: I've always used the full traveler, both sides, even in medium air. I have never been able to get the boat going when the sheet was clipped in the middle. Of course, I've always had a fairly full sail. I can remember many events when the thing would catch in the middle and the boat would stop—something was wrong. I would look around and there it was, the traveler stuck in the middle. I would push it to leeward

and the boat would go again.
W: How about your gooseneck? Do you play with that?
O: Well, in light and medium air, I always move it forward. It seems to let the boat point a lot better. With my old stretched sail, in seas and 10 to 15 knots of wind, I always kept it within two or three inches of the aft clip. With the new Fogh sail, it seems to go better with the gooseneck further aft, but it's awfully easy to get a lee helm. I had it too far back this summer and a few times I let go of the helm and instead of coming up, the boat bore off. With the old Ratsey sail I never had that situation.
W: How tight do you keep your foot and your luff? Do you play with the outhauls?
O: Not when I'm racing. I set them up with the classic adjustments. If it's blowing, I honk the luff down as far as I can. In very, very light air, I adjust it fairly tightly—not really tight, but so that there are no wrinkles. Then in medium air I adjust it somewhere in between. The new sail is so full that letting the outhaul loose so that there are scallops along the luff doesn't make sense anymore.

I have never played with stretching the foot. I tighten it just enough so that there are no wrinkles under sail.
W: One more question on the beat. How do you tack?
O: In light air, some sort of roll tack works fairly well. But in heavy air, I come around so fast it's not necessary. I try playing the waves so that I don't get stopped by one as I'm coming about. It's a question of judgment. Every third

or fourth wave is a biggy, so once it's past, that's the time to tack.

W: Do you look for a flat place in the water, or do you try to pirouette around on top of the wave?

O: The Sunfish doesn't tack that fast. I think in a tack you're certainly going to be involved in a couple of waves. It's not the way you can turn on top of a mogul in skiing. You turn on one wave, but you're probably going to hit one or two more. After I get hit by a big wave, I try to get my speed up and then tack. I look for a flat part between waves.

W: What about your centerboard and rudder?

O: The Sunfish has too small a board and rudder for the sail area, so the boat tends to stall out. Once you get a high degree of water flow on the leading edge of the centerboard, the boat stalls if you have a sharp leading edge. So the blunt two-to-one ellipse leading edge of the old board makes a world of difference. Especially in situations where you are over-powered. In light air, even light to medium air, the leading edge doesn't make that much difference.

All the boards Alcort has made for the last 15 years are useless, I think. You have to use Bondo body putty, and build them up. We made a template for the leading edge. With that, you can grind down the Bondo to get a perfect ellipse. I think it's very important to have a blunt leading edge, but there is an optimum airfoil shape. Of course you only have a little over an inch to play with, but a two-to-one ellipse is very close. I went to a NACA airfoil book one day and found that what we have on the board is about as close as you can get to an optimum leading edge for good stall resistance.

A blunt rudder is also awfully important. Unless a person has some aerodynamic engineering background, he thinks sharp is nice—it slices through the water. He doesn't realize that the boat is going to go sideways.

W: What about kinetics? You were talking about moving around in the boat, getting the bow up and all that.

O: I read an article on it once. I've been trying to practice it for years and still can't get it down. The classic thing is to get the boat on a plane by giving it a couple of pumps and then veering off down the wave. I have not had much luck at it, especially on reaches. To windward I do fine, but on the reaches I've always had guys go by me.

W: I think that's as much a function of weight as anything.

O: Well, I don't know. In Sardinia in one race I was first to the windward mark by 50 yards and the second guy was Chapin. He passed me on the reach and had 50 yards on *me* at the next mark. We weigh about the same. It's a very delicate thing, the right pump and you get the boat going and surf down the wave. He had it, and I didn't.

The master whom I've watched and marveled at is Catalano. He's all over the race course and able to veer off and keep the boat going downhill for a higher percentage of the time than anybody else. It obviously makes yards of difference. It's a real art and I think it just takes a lot of time and practice to be able to master it.

W: Do you use the halyard end as a vang?

O: Only to pull the gooseneck down when it

blows. With the new sail being as full as it is, I think that it makes a big difference to pull the gooseneck down when it blows, to try to flatten the sail out. There aren't that many things you can do to flatten out the sail.

W: How about on the run? What kind of things do you do?

O: I think it is very effective to sit to windward and sail with an extreme heel, almost capsizing, without dragging your butt in the water. That delicate balance of almost going over, to reduce the wetted area and get the sail upright, makes a big difference. Almost everybody does it, but not to the extreme of almost capsizing. I think the last six inches or whatever makes a difference.

W: Do you worry about the weight of your boat?

O: I think weight is important and very little has been written about it. It should be pointed out that the class has no hull weight limits, although there is a rule that you can't take flotation out of the hull. You can race any weight boat that you can find.

I remember one year we weighed our boats at Bolton Lake. We weighed probably 25 boats. They ranged from my boat, which was the heaviest at 159 pounds, to Major Hall's at 117 pounds. Both boats were dry, factory-built and there had been no adjustments—yet there was a 40-pound difference. If you've ever picked up a water bag weighing 15 pounds and put it on your shoulders, you know it feels like a ton of bricks. People are going around with 20, 30, 40 excess pounds in their boats. That's just dead weight.

W: I had one super-light boat that was real loose and I couldn't go anywhere, especially in heavy air.

O: I went through that too. One year at Madison, both my vertical foam blocks fell down. I looked in through my port and I could see the bottom of the boat flexing up and down a couple of inches. I never went so fast in my life. I did just super. There were waves, it was blowing, but the boat went tremendously. I thought it was going to break. I'd come off a wave and the whole boat would shake, but it went like hell.

I'd just like to point out that there's a variety in boat weight. Someone who's a little on the heavy side should shop around. There are a lot of light boats out there.

There are all kinds of methods for drying your boat out. People may realize that they have a leaker and think that it's tough to fix. But there's no trick. You can certainly get the weight down to where it's supposed to be. Just blow into the drain port with a vacuum cleaner, track down the leaks and plug them up. There's no reason why the thing has to leak. Once you get the thing to stop leaking, open the inspection port and leave the boat in the sun to dry out.

I've used desiccant, which absorbs about its own weight in water. You can buy these bags of silica gel and stick them in the hull and then close up the hull. Later you pick the bag up and it's twice the original size. It will suck the boat absolutely dry. It's now being sold for cruising boats to keep moisture out of lockers and things After it soaks up the water, you stick the bag in the oven for 12 hours or something like that.

It dries out and you can use it again and again. At major events, I always dry out the hull. I put the desiccant in at night and then take it out in the morning and the boat is as dry as can be.

W: Any other boat tuning ideas?

O: Another thing on the centerboards. The class rules give the tolerances, which are usually plus or minus a quarter of an inch. According to Steve Baker, that really means that if you have a board cut to factory specifications, you'll find that you're a quarter-inch under the max. That quarter inch can make a big difference. So in working on the leading and trailing edges, the name of the game is to bring them up to the maximum.

I have a tip on the bailer. I've got a little gismo in there that really works well. The standard plastic bailer with the cap on the top doesn't fit well. It leaks and is very difficult to undo when you are on a plane. I've hooked up a plumber's half-inch faucet washer on the end of a string and it fits in the hole exactly. So you can go to windward without the bailer open. As you veer off on the reach, even when you are hiking, you can just reach over, pull the string and your bailer is open.

W: You don't kick it loose when you tack?

O: No, I haven't had any problems. I drilled a hole in the back of the cockpit and the line is long enough to hang back into the storage well.

W: How do you like to start?

O: In the big regattas, a start I've been able to get away with is a late start at the committee boat. It seems that at big events, like the North Americans and the Worlds, people are a little nervous and tend to get up to the line early. They usually go for the middle of the line or try to be up on it. I just kind of hold back, stay in a barging position at the committee boat end of the line, and come in late. I've got speed. Chances are a hole will develop and I can go on to port tack. I might sacrifice five to 10 seconds, but within about 30 seconds after the start, I have free air and can tack. That's the tactic I usually use and I've had tremendous luck with it.

W: Thanks for your help, Paul.

Nat Philbrick and the trophy he garnered after winning the Sunfish North American Championship in 1978.

Nat Philbrick

Nat Philbrick comes from a 100-percent Sunfish family. Father Tom and mother Marianne win regularly in Senior Olympic competition. Brother Sam has done well in the big competitions, including a ninth at the Worlds in 1979 and an 11th at the 1978 North Americans. Nat's wife Melissa was second at the Women's North Americans in 1981. Nat himself was North American Champion in 1978, and was fifth at the Worlds in 1978 and fourth in 1979. At this writing, he is Assistant Editor of *Yacht Racing/ Cruising.* (Another Sunfish North American Champion, Major Hall, was Editor for several years.)

White: Let's get into the details of how you make a Sunfish go to windward.
Philbrick: The primary factor in a Sunfish, compared to other boats, is the fact that it has a chine. So you want to sail it heeled a little more than you would most boats. In light air, I find that speed to weather is a function of making sure you have enough helm. If a puff lets up, you have to come in; when you anticipate a puff, you have to go out. The boat is so underpowered that if you are not attuned to what's happening with the wind, you can really stall out quickly. A lot of Sunfish sailors seem to just sit there and lose track of that aspect of sailing.

In heavy air, it's a lot like any other boat. You have to play the mainsheet and steer around the waves.
W: Talk about playing the mainsheet.
P: In light air, I usually hold it above the Harken. I pull it in if I'm trying to head up and

let it out if I'm trying to come down. When in doubt, I let it out. I play with about four-inch lengths of sheet and try not to steer too much.

W: Would you consider yourself a pincher or a footer?

P: It's a fine line. I always watch how I am sailing in relation to the rest of the fleet. At times, I'll try to pinch a little bit more, but it depends what kind of shift I'm sailing into. If I expect a header, I'll foot off. If it's a lay line situation and I want to stay above somebody, I'll pinch. I try to keep my options open. If I find myself footing all the time, it's because I can't point—and vice versa.

I keep my sail a little flatter than most people. I usually have the outhauls pretty tight, even in light to medium air. It's easier for a boat to stall out with a flatter sail, so you have to be careful.

W: How about the bridle?

P: I used to just clip the sheet in the middle. Now I'm using the "Hoyt effect" more and more. This means clipping the sheet to the port side of the bridle. It's named after Garry Hoyt, first World Sunfish Champion, who introduced the idea. I'm beginning to let the sheet slide when I'm on port tack, as well as on starboard tack. You know, taping the bridle so the sheet slides from side to side.

W: How about the gooseneck?

P: That's a very critical adjustment. In light air, I put it far forward, almost approaching the sail clip. It's a function of how much helm I have. If I'm not pointing, I move the gooseneck forward. In my sailing career, I've had a tendency to move it farther and farther forward. It seems to help pointing a lot. As conditions get heavier and I can't hold the boat down, I move the gooseneck aft. Before I used the Jens rig, I'd bring the gooseneck way back. It was just about the only way of depowering. Then, with the Jens rig, I discovered you have to move the gooseneck way forward. That was something I had to find out for myself. I think some people don't move it around as much.

W: How do you steer through waves? Do you head up going up the wave and bear off going down?

P: Yes, that's standard. I just make sure I have plenty of speed to do any kind of maneuver I want to do and I don't head up if I'm not going fast enough.

W: What about tacking? Do you feel roll tacking is important?

P: Yes, particularly in light air. In heavy air, if you don't time it right and don't use your body right, you can get in irons. It's a little more important on a Sunfish than it is on a lot of other boats, just because of that.

W: Do you face forward or aft when you tack?

P: I face forward.

W: How about telltales?

P: I usually use tape-recording tape on wires on the upper spar.

W: How about reaches? How do you sail them?

P: I use a lot of body movement and play the sail constantly. I always check to see how I'm steering in relation to the rhumb line, checking that I'm not getting too far to weather. I like to leave the rest of the fleet alone and go for it.

W: Try to describe the kinetics you use. I know it's sort of like trying to tell people how to ride

a bike, but give it a shot.

P: Okay. The kinetics I use are really to help steer the boat. In a lull, when the boat goes flat and I want to initiate a move to weather, I come in. I come in and head up just to help the boat through a stagnant period, to keep the wind flow over the sails. If the wind comes up again, I go out, flatten the boat down and use the opportunity to bring myself back down towards the rhumb line.

W: Do you do much pumping to get on a plane?

P: It really depends on the wave conditions. If there are a lot of waves, yes, I do an awful lot of pumping. You really have to, in order to make sure the boat's jumping on every possible wave. Sometimes it can be an almost continual process, which is very exhausting.

W: Okay, let's get on to the run. Tell me about how you run.

P: Particularly in heavy air and waves, you can go a lot faster than everybody else by keeping the boat right on the edge, heeling to weather. By playing that mainsail so that it's really cocked up, you can catch waves more easily and sustain a plane much better. The whole rig is more balanced when you're right on the edge.

W: How do you keep the bow from burying?

P: That's a tough one, because the fastest point of sail will often be just before the bow digs in. It may take a few pitchpoles to discover just when you have to jump back. Sometimes, I yank hard on the sheet, bear off dramatically and come out of it. It's often easier if you just head up out of it. If it's really looking like it's a dive, you have to do something quickly.

W: How do you like to start?

P: Fairly conservatively. I want the ability to keep up close to the line. It's more important to me to have free air and options than going for a great start. Usually, I'm somewhere around the favored end.

W: What about in a great big fleet, like at the Worlds?

P: The lines are long, but they are usually pretty good. If there is a favored side, it's good to get in that area—but just make sure you're in the first row. If you're not, then it's a disaster. I like to keep my options open so I can clear my air and get to the favored side.

W: What about your rudder and board? Do you do anything to them?

P: Actually, I hate to say this, but my father does everything to our boards. That's his hobby and he spends all his winter just doing boards and rudders. He's a foil expert. He does amazing things to the foils. He's turned the original new-style boards, the very small ones, into the new Barrington boards. They just grow to his touch. He blunts the leading edge and has an elaborate system of gel coating and painting. He has experimental boards that he plays with to see what happens.

W: How about the tiller and the hiking stick?

P: I add a little glass around the tiller where the bridle chafes. I guess it's legal to have a universal joint now, but I haven't gotten to that point yet. I use a brass ring at the end of the tiller extension.

W: Anything special on the sheet?

P: I just use a standard Dacron line. When I was organized, I had two sheets. One for light or moderate air and a thicker one for heavier air. I think it is a mistake to have one that's too long. In heavy air, if you jibe and lose the sheet and the knot is out to far, you can dump to weather.

W: Too short a sheet isn't good either. What about the bottom? Do you do anything with that?

P: During the season, I'll wash it every now and then. Before a big regatta, I'll sand it and fill in the dents. I sand with standard #400 or #600 sandpaper and use Marinetex to fill in the dents.

W: Let's talk about sails.

P: Okay. I think the new sails look great compared to the old ones. My first experience with the new sail was this summer and it seemed to be just as fast as the old one without doing anything dramatically different. Originally, it had a little more fullness than I wanted. I don't adjust my outhauls that much. I try to get a nice shape for what I think the condtions will be for that race. My upper spar is always a little tighter than my lower spar. I use lines instead of sail clips on the last two grommets on each spar, so I can adjust my leech.

W: Do you worry about weight and stiffness? Which is the most important?

P: In a Sunfish I think that stiffness is by far the most important thing. I'm always amazed how weight doesn't seem to make that much difference. I used to have a boat that was 30 pounds heavier than the one I have now and it didn't seem much different. In heavy-air planing, the lighter boat seemed to be a bit quicker. But in anything else, I couldn't tell the difference.

W: Do you fill in the trunk much? Do you worry about vibration?

P: Yes. I get the trunk as smooth as possible. If there's vibration, there's usually something wrong with the board. It may just be a little ding. Or it's not absolutely straight—there's a twist in it or something.

W: Do you do any particular exercises to get in shape?

P: I run a little bit, but I wouldn't say it's really for sailing. The only reason I was in shape in 1978 was because I was sailing all the time. For me, arm strength is the first thing that goes. If I were going to be competitive, racing in the Worlds, I know I would have to do a lot of upper-body exercise.

W: How about weight? Do you ever wear weight?

P: The most I would put on is four sweat shirts. I'm morally against water jackets and things like that. They hurt my back—I think that's where my morals come from. I don't get mad if somebody else uses them. More power to them. I just don't think it's worth it.

W: How about clothing? Do you wear padding under those thighs?

P: I would now if I had to do a lot of racing. When I'm sailing a lot in the Sunfish, I guess the calluses are there. I'll maybe wear an extra pair of shorts. I find that what is really important is the texture of what you have on your rear end. You want something you are able to push against. You don't want something too slippery and you don't want something that's like sandpaper.

W: Thanks, Nat.

Cor van Aanholt of Holland was World Champion in 1980, runner-up in 1979, and third in 1981.

Cor van Aanholt

Cor van Aanholt, Sunfish World Champion, started sailing in 1971 at the age of 12. He and his brother began racing in the Flits class (an 11½-foot wooden two-man boat popular in the northern Netherlands for juniors up to age 18). They won the Flits Nationals twice in a row when Cor was 13 and 14.

The next year, Cor crewed for his older brother Peter in a Flying Junior. Cor was tactician and Peter handled the helm and kept the boat moving. Cor was impatient crewing, so he looked around for a good single-hander. He said that although he didn't particularly like the looks of the Laser, he sailed one anyway because they were popular.

At age 17, he won the famous Kielwoche in Kiel, West Germany (Kiel Week was used in 1980 by the nations boycotting the Olympics as a substitute event). This qualified him for the 1976 Laser Worlds, in which he finished sixth. He placed very well in several major Laser championships and placed second in the 1979 Sunfish Worlds in Medemblik, Holland.

He arrived in Aruba for the 1980 Sunfish Worlds two-and-a-half weeks prior to the event. He said that he often does this to acclimatize himself to the differences in time, weather and food. He sailed only three times on a borrowed Sunfish—he said that he doesn't think sailing is the best way to psych up for a regatta. He prefers to see the area or country he is visiting. This sightseeing gives him plenty of time for relaxation, which he considers essential to good sailing.

Like most good sailors, Cor always arrives at

the starting area at least 10 minutes before the start. He checks the wind and wave conditions and makes last-minute adjustments to his rig.

Cor plans to continue sailing the Sunfish, especially since he is now a dealer.

White: How did you get interested in Sunfish?
Cor: The Dutch Sunfish Association invited me to the World Championships in Medemblik in 1979. I thought it was very interesting to start sailing Sunfish, because they are quite similar to the Lasers. I went to this championship and was amazed at how nice a class it was. The boat is easy to sail and still nice with tactics and things like that.
W: Let's talk about how you sail. How do you make the Sunfish go to windward?
C: It's very hard for me to go to windward in light wind, because it is so important to know exactly the correct trim of the boat. For that you need a lot of practice. When there is a lot of wind, there is a lot of fighting to it. I think it's easier to sail a boat you've never sailed before when there is a lot of wind, because trimming the sail is much easier. You can flatten it out, you can use the vang and other things that are quite similar in all boats. That's why it was so easy for me in my first World Championship. We had four of the six races with a lot of wind and in those four races, I had very nice results.
W: Do you point or foot?
C: I think I foot. I veer off more than the others do. That was very apparent at the first Worlds I sailed in Medemblik. I went very, very low compared with Fries and Chapin. They sailed

much higher, but because I went faster, I could take the shifts faster. That was quite an advantage because the wind was shifting a lot.
W: Did you use the compass a lot? Or were you able to tell by the shore?
C: I never sail with a compass. Never. I haven't even got one. I think it's better to look at the other competitors because they can give you an indication of all the wind shifts even better than a compass can. You're not sailing against the wind; you're sailing against other competitors. I think if you look at the other competitors, you can observe two things at once: the wind shifts and the tactics.
W: How do you set up your bridle? How do you put your sheet on the bridle? Do you use the rope bridle?
C: For me it's very difficult because I hardly know the class. I know quite a bit about tactics, but the Sunfish itself is pretty new to me. I prefer the rope bridle because I want to put the traveler pretty low, so tight that when there is not much wind it works a little bit as a downhaul.
W: How tight do you have your foot and your luff?
C: That's difficult—I think not that loose. If you put it too loose you get wrinkles in your sail and I don't like that. The more wind I get, the tighter I make my outhaul.
W: How about body kinetics to windward?
C: I think they're very important in Sunfish and Lasers and all these very light boats. Compared to the total weight of the boat, the sailor is about 50 percent of it, and that's quite a lot. So I think it's very important to move your body. As you go up a wave, you have to put

your body to the front of the boat, and when you're on the top, you move your body back again. I go forward and backward, in and out, and I don't know exactly how I do it. I think I make a circle with my shoulders. If I am going up the wave, I am hiking out a little bit and I'm going forward with my shoulders. As I go down the wave I go back and in again. I think it turns out to be a circle.

W: How do you tack in waves? How do you pick the time to tack?

C: I try to start tacking when the wave is coming and finish my tack when I am sailing down the wave.

W: You're tacking across the crest of the wave?

C: Yes, on top of the wave. I try to make something like a roll tack, but it's hard to do. If the waves are different sizes, you should try to tack on the flattest possible spot. But if you have to tack, well, tack on top of the wave. It's better to have a good technique for tacking on waves than waiting to tack for 20 meters and losing your position.

W: Do you use telltales at all?

C: No, never. They mix me up too much. They might be very good for training, but I wouldn't use them in a regatta.

W: Let's get on to the next point of sailing. Tell me about your reaching technique and tactics.

C: Usually I try to make a straight line from one mark to the other. I remember I once read something by a guy who won the Sunfish Worlds. He wrote about surfing on a wave on a normal surfboard, and actually that's the same way you have to sail a Sunfish. It was very helpful.

W: Was that Garry Hoyt's Go for the Gold?

C: Yes! That's the only book I've ever read about sailing. It was a good book and I learned a lot about surfing on waves in small boats.

W: You're going downhill all the time?

C: Yes. If you really work on it, I think you can surf down the whole reach. You need a lot of training for that or else all the waves would look the same. If you're working on it and if you've been training on the waves for a while, then you see the differences. Then you can take the waves you like.

W: Do you find it helps to pump the sail?

C: It's harder than on Lasers because when you pump, you have the forward part of the sail, the part in front of the mast, working against you. You do need the help of a good pump to get planing. It's hard for me to pump in the right way, but that's lack of training. I never trained in Sunfish at all. The only times I sailed the Sunfish was in the regattas. I think altogether I've sailed Sunfish about 28 times.

W: How about on the run? Do you do anything different on the run than on the reach?

C: I don't think so. I like to sail by the lee. I think you can get a lot of advantage out of that. If you sail a little bit on the lee, it seems to be easier to catch a wave and to keep on surfing.

W: Do you try to jibe on shifts?

C: Yes, I try. I also try to get a little bit away from the field of boats. Fifty percent of the time I do it, it turns out to be equal. But the other 50 percent of the time, I think I have a small advantage. I try to keep a clear wind.

W: How about kinetics on the reach and the run?

C: Again, very important. As I said, it's very important to move your body forward and backward as you go upwind. It's also very important when you're on a run or a reach. As I read in the book, *Go for the Gold*, it's just as if you're surfing down a wave on a surfboard. If you want to catch a wave, you must be in the front of the boat at the moment you catch it. Then you have to move backward. It's not a quick jump in the boat—it's just a changing of weight.

W: How about starting tactics? How do you like to start?

C: Actually I don't care about other people. I just try to take the best place and go off. I think you need good boat handling and you must be sure of yourself. I prefer to start on the left side of the line. At Medemblik I was always to the left, but this was because I had a lot of speed when I footed. I found that at the right side of the line, I would be in everybody's wind. I also had to tack immediately if I started at the right side of the line and that was not always possible. If I started at the lowest end I could make good speed, take a nice shift and pass in front of the fleet.

W: Do you do any training—physical exercises?

C: At the moment I do too little, but usually I do a lot of running. When I'm really trying hard to win something, I run three or four times a week, about 10 kilometers. After that I do some physical fitness things like push-ups and sit-ups. I also do something like meditation where I am moving my body and stretching it. Altogether, it takes about one-and-a-quarter hours. I play a lot of squash and do other sports like water skiing and surfing. I sailed the Dutch windsurfing championships and won.

If you do a lot of sports and are doing extra work on your muscles, especially your stomach muscles, I think that's enough. You have to be very, very fit to sail the Sunfish in heavy wind. It's very important in all classes where the boat is pretty light compared to the body. You really have to work hard.

W: Do you wear weight?

C: A bit. I only wear wet sweat shirts—about three or four kilos (six-and-one-half to nine pounds).

W: Many thanks, Cor.

Action at the jibe mark at the 1973
Martinique Worlds.

10 *River Racing*

When Jack Evans and I were looking for a new kind of competition for Sunfish, I remembered a cruise with my sons the previous summer from Windsor Locks, Connecticut, to Old Saybrook, a distance of 52 miles. We camped out overnight at Hurd State Park, about two-thirds of the way down. Based on that experience, Jack and I invented the Long-Distance Down-the-Connecticut-River Mixed Doubles Championship, a two-day race, and made it a series of races so boats would not get spread too far apart. The rules required that you carried your own camping equipment and lunches, but Alcort supplied dinner and breakfast. It was spur-of-the-moment, and we ran the first of these annual races three weeks later. There were six boats, and we all had a wonderful time.

The next year, there were 36 boats. Since then, Alcort has had to limit the entries to 75, for safety's sake. One of these days, we figure, a squall will come whipping up the river, flatten everybody, and many will need help from chase boats. Every year, Alcort manages to lure five stinkpotters to bring their outboards along, for safety purposes. Interestingly, most of the competitors in the Connecticut River race are rugged outdoorsy types rather than the hotshots you will find on the regatta circuit. But every year, one or two of the good ones—real lovers of sailing—show up and, of course, clean up. Actually, racing is very informal and the winners are, with good nature, chided for trying too hard.

Since that first Connecticut River race, other point-to-point races have been launched: 'Round Key West in Florida, 'Round Bermuda out there at the northern tip of THE Triangle, and 'Round Cape Ann at the northeast corner of Massachusetts. There is also a 'Round Shelter Island race out in the crotch of Long Island, New York, called "The World's Longest Sunfish Race." It's a day-long affair, and probably still is the longest, if you eliminate the Connecticut River race because that's a series of races.

Even though river racing is supposed to be relaxed, and there is some social stigma to trying too hard, there are ways to make a boat sail fast down a river, and I wrote down some thoughts about them—things I've learned on the way to six victories in the Connecticut River race. Some of those things are helpful in racing on small lakes, too.

A great deal has been written about round-the-buoys sailboat racing, meteorology and how to predict wind shifts. Much has been written about tides and currents, as well, since many round-the-buoys courses are set in tide waters. But not too much has been written about sailing fast down a river, since river racing in small sailboats is relatively new. In fact, as far as we know, it was pioneered by the Sunfish Class on the Connecticut River.

River racing, at least so far, is a relatively low-key affair. One of the published rules for the "Great Connecticut River Race" is "Don't take it too seriously." Starts, as described by Joanne Fishman of the *New York Times*, tend to be "a floating version of bumper cars" where the rules are observed if possible, but if it's not possible . . . well, in the first nine years of the Connecticut River race, there were no protests.

The 10th Connecticut River race was sailed in 1982. Here the vanguard of the 75-boat fleet passes Goodspeed Opera House in East Haddam.

However, once the tangle of the start is sorted out, it becomes a challenge to sail the fastest possible course down the river. The sailor's mind must be an adaptable computer, with two major sources of input—wind and current. It is possible to get down the river by just letting the current sweep you along, with the wind helping most of the time. But the secret of getting down the river first is to find the best combination of wind and current.

This type of sailing requires a certain kind of adaptability not usually called upon in round-the-buoys racing. Every bend in the river seems to bring a brand new set of conditions. The fastest part of the current will suddenly have shifted to the other shore, and the wind will have swung 45 or 90 degrees or disappeared altogether. Actually, if there is a current, the wind never totally disappears, unless it is blowing in the same direction and at the same speed as the current. But in a flat calm, a current will sweep you along, creating a one-knot breeze if it is a one-knot current.

This phenomenon raises an interesting point. In a flat calm, is it faster just to sit in the fastest part of the current and drift downstream, or should you beat into the wind created by the current? A little reflection should provide the right answer. If you just drift, you will drift at the speed of the current. If you beat, you will add the speed made good to windward to that of the current, and get there faster.

But back to the current. Where does it flow fastest? In carving out river beds, currents seem to carom from one bank to the other around the bend, carving the deepest channel on the outside of each curve. Water flows fastest in the deepest part of the river, since there is less friction from the bottom. The fastest current is usually on the outside of each bend. However, this is one rule that Mother Nature sometimes likes to break. A river bottom may be formed by other than the action of the water—a shift in geological strata, for instance—and the current may hug the inside of the curve. This can happen in a gorge, or where there is cliff on one bank and flat land on the other. But not always. If you really want to know, study the charts of the river, if there are any. There's no guarantee that the deepest part of the channel will stay where the chartmakers put it, but it is better than guessing. Many rivers, of course, have channels dredged for commercial traffic, and you're pretty safe following these.

Sometimes bridge pilings or jetties can produce interesting effects on the current. Where a river piling splits the water, the current is often quite fast. There is almost a jet stream, and if you catch it, you can get a jump of several boat lengths. However, you have to catch it at the right angle, because there is often a back eddy at the downstream end, and if you get caught in that, it's like hitting a stone wall, especially if there is no wind. There are often back eddies close to shore, as well, and an occasional sailor gets caught in one if he is trying to sneak too close to shore to get a favorable wind slant.

There is another phenomenon to watch for, this one on tidal rivers. The current may be downstream for seven or eight or nine hours, then imperceptibly stop and start flowing

Sailors find more uses for Sunfish halyards than Indians did for birch bark. The Connecticut River race.

The mother/daughter team of Linda and Rhoda Babcock fully rigged for the Great Long-Distance Down-the-Connecticut River Race.

168

upstream as the tide comes in. It is quite possible for it to flow upstream on one side of a wide river, while flowing downstream on the other. If you are racing downstream, you know where you want to be.

So you've gotten out the charts, and talked to some riverboat pilots, and you are pretty sure you know where the current will be on every stretch of the river? Don't bank on it. Watch the river. If you are in the middle, and the water seems to be flowing faster on one side or the other, you may want to get over into the faster current, even though the chart says it shouldn't be faster over there. Trust your eyes. You can tell by the action of the water, or the flotsam and jetsam that usually accompanies you downstream. Of course, if you have a nice 12-knot breeze on the beam, and you are planing down the river at an exhilarating clip, actually seeing differences in current speed becomes pretty difficult. But then, in that kind of breeze, you are probably better off playing the wind rather than the current.

And that brings in the other major factor in river sailing—the wind. Just as the current is seldom the same speed across the width of the river, so is the wind. Both direction and force can vary considerably from one side of the river to the other, and you can pretty well count on its being different 200 yards downstream. So while you want to be very conscious of the current, especially in very light air, you have to try to dope out the wind simultaneously.

Every sailor knows that the shoreline does funny things with the wind sometimes. These tricks are compounded on the river. If the banks are high, or the trees are thick, the river can become a wind tunnel, bending the wind up or downstream. It is often possible to stay on one tack a lot longer than you might think possible, because the wind is bending around a curve and lifting you. It is this phenomenon that can often trap you in a back eddy, if you try to ride that lift too far inshore. On the other hand, if you don't ride in that lift to the last possible second, your competitor may—and get a jump of several boat lengths on you.

Even more than on a lake, interesting local breezes can spring up from temperature differentials between the land and the water. It pays to watch the surface of the water, not only for currents, but also for cat's paws of wind, especially in light air. Even relatively minor differences in temperature from one side of the river to the other, or from the water to the land, or from one stretch of river to another can cause thermal breezes to spring up. It is probably impossible to predict them. But it is important to watch for them.

Breezes blowing across a stretch of river can also do some interesting things. If the wind is blowing off a higher bank toward a lower bank, it is almost always best to be close to the lower bank, since the higher bank will have a blanketing effect. But cross-stream winds can give you more subtle problems. In rolling terrain, especially, the wind seems to be able to skip across the water. It may "bounce" in the middle, or close to one side or the other. Or it may skip twice, leaving a sort of dead air tunnel down the middle of the river! More troublesome still, the pattern does not remain constant, varying

unpredictably as you go downstream, or even as the actual wind strength increases or decreases. You can see a boat a hundred yards ahead that seems to be right in the area where the wind is bouncing hardest, and by the time you get there, it is bouncing somewhere else. This bouncing of the wind takes place on open water, too—it is apparently the cause of localized gusts—but on the river it is confusion compounded.

Whether you are racing or not, sailing a river is a fascinating exercise in piloting. One point to remember—it is great fun to sail from a point upstream to a point downstream if there is somebody there to pick you up. But if you have to get back to your launching point, a good rule to follow is to sail against the current for the first leg. Then, if the wind quits, you will at least drift back on the current to your home port.

11 *The Cruising Sunfish*

Many years ago, when I had just bought my first Sailfish, I was interviewing a salesman in my office and told him about it. He said, "Oh, you'll have a ball with your Sailfish. Every summer, my son and I cruise around the Elizabeth Islands for a week on ours." Now the Elizabeth Islands are the southern boundary of Buzzards Bay, and I had sailed on Buzzards Bay. It can be a pretty wild piece of water. The idea of cruising on a Sailfish, lugging along your camping gear, sitting for hours on a bouncing board, sounds like an exercise in masochism. To do it on the stormy waters of Buzzards Bay and Vineyard Sound sounds suicidal.

I decided to cruise the Connecticut River instead and a few years later, talked two of my sons into trying it with me. They were 11 and 13, and sailed one Sunfish with just a few things on board wrapped in light plastic bags—sweaters and foul-weather gear, lunch, and other things they might need on the water. I sailed another, with most of the camping gear and clothing wrapped in plastic garbage bags and lashed on deck.

We sailed the Connecticut River from Windsor Locks to Long Island Sound, a distance of roughly 52 miles, in two days. We camped out at Hurd State Park in East Haddam. What is remarkable to me about that trip is that we had a wonderful time even though we had only one small pup tent, it was a damp and chilly April weekend, and it drizzled most of the time we were in camp. Then, on the last leg into Essex, the wind started picking up, blowing straight upriver, and the boys capsized. I fished them out of the river, along with several floating plastic bags, righted their boat, lowered the rig, tied it on the deck, and took them in tow.

Unfortunately, the Sunfish is not designed for towing things. There was a steep chop, the current was flowing upriver, and we weren't making much headway. So I lowered my sail, too, shipped the rowing rig I had devised, and rowed the last four miles with them in tow. We arrived at the ramp under the I-95 bridge in Old Saybrook in the late afternoon, tired, only a little damp, and happy. As I said, we had a good time. I was hooked, and have done the trip several times since, just for fun.

The important thing about cruising on the Sunfish is to remember that it's very much like back-packing through water up to your neck. You want to travel light, and you want to travel waterproof. Over the years, we have found that carrying the gear between the daggerboard and the mast seems to give the boat its best balance, and leaves enough sitting room for two people to be fairly comfortable. Wrap your gear in small plastic bags—doubled up for an extra margin of safety—and then stuff all those into large heavy-walled garbage or lawn bags. I use at least two, and usually three, stuffing the first bag mouth down into the second, and so on. Then you can strap the large bags onto the deck with two or three shock cords of the kind used to hold luggage to a car roof rack. I have capsized with this rig, and everything somehow stayed dry. Nevertheless, the plastic bags are not very strong, and can sometimes get torn, so I have taken to stuffing packed plastic bags into canvas duffel bags, just for abrasion resistance.

With this gear, of course, you have to carry

James Lee Meadows sailed from Miami to Boston. He obviously traveled light.

the sail a little higher than you do when you are racing, but then, who's racing?

I have never heard of anybody trying to overnight on a Sunfish. I wouldn't plan it unless you don't care about sleeping. But putting into shore every night, and pitching a tent or sleeping under the stars, can be a very relaxing way to spend a week or so. In 1977, a fellow named James Lee Meadows sailed from Florida to Boston on a Sunfish, and had a wonderful time. He was in no hurry, and occasionally stayed for weeks at a time if he found a particularly hospitable spot on shore. But it's not the sort of thing you should do unless you know how to handle a Sunfish.

A few years earlier, a man and his son cruised Long Island Sound for a week in this manner, and wrote a glowing account of their trip for *Scuttlebutt*, the original Sunfish newsletter. The next year, however, they decided to continue up the coast to Buzzards Bay, and one day they found themselves out in the middle of that choppy body of water, trying to tack against a stiff wind. They finally gave up and headed back to shore downwind and wrote Alcort to let them know that cruising in the Sunfish was dangerous on open water. It certainly can be. But note that they were able to sail out of trouble, even though they were not very experienced. Just remember that two people plus sailing gear on a Sunfish is a pretty heavy load, and I can imagine that it is pretty hard to go to windward under these conditions.

If you are doing your camping/cruising on tidal waters, it's important to remember those tides. In fact, it's important to remember tides

172

when you are sailing at regattas off the beach. More than one Sunfish has sailed away from a regatta without any skipper when the incoming tide floated it free. At a regatta, that's at most a matter of embarrassment. If you are camping/sailing on your own, you could be marooned. Being a castaway has certain romantic overtones, but I have a hunch that most people who have lived through it would just as soon not repeat the experience.

It is usually easy enough to tell where the high tide normally stops. There is usually a lot of dead or dying seaweed and flotsam and the like clearly drawing a line at the high tide mark. Drag the boat above that level. And, just to make sure, tie a line from the boat to something on the beach. Of course, you will want to make camp above this mark. One of the least comfortable things that can happen to you is to get your blanket roll or sleeping bag wet . . . especially when you are sleeping in it.

River currents and tidal currents can often fool you. On a tidal river, the current will mostly take you downstream, but for some part of the day, the current will actually be flowing upstream. On a river, that's not likely to get you into trouble. But on coastal waters, currents can really throw you off course, especially if visibility is restricted by fog or rain. You may think you are sailing close to shore, and find that you are really so far out of line that, when visibility returns, you have lost sight of land. So it's a good idea to study a good current table before you start your trip and to know when the currents are changing and which way they flow.

If it is at all possible that you will stray out of sight of land, make sure you take along a compass. Sometimes you will wish that you had an anchor along. The smallest Danforth is more than adequate for a Sunfish, with 3/16th nylon line. It is the most awkward gear I recommend taking along, but if you want to hold your own against the current when the wind is very light, you will be glad it's along. The alternative is a paddle, which has a lot more uses than helping you hold your own against current. It can help you get where you are going in a calm, and can serve as a crutch on which to prop the side of the boat when you drain it. And it can serve as a tent pole. So the anchor is a luxury; the paddle is not. Take a paddle.

I have heard of people navigating by road map, but it sure is a chancy way to cruise. I like to know where I am all the time, and keep an open chart close at hand. Of course, in a Sunfish, you don't have many places to keep it, and the government doesn't print its charts on waterproof paper. One of the best wrinkles is to cut the chart up into 8½″ x 11″ pieces, being careful to code all four sides, so you know how to find the next piece when you sail off the edge. Then you keep these pieces, book fashion, in one of those 9″ x 12″ clear plastic bags with a ziploc top. You can tape these to the deck. At regattas, I often do that, to hold the local chart or diagram of the race course along with race instructions.

Of course, if you are cruising a river or small lake, it's usually easy enough to get to shore and ask where you are. But if you are sailing in relatively open water, it's a lot more healthy to *know* where you are.

Most of the time, when you are camping/cruising, you will be putting up overnight on sandy beaches. In many ways, camping on sand is great. You can dig a little hole and make a fire in it and not worry that you're going to set the forest ablaze. You can dig out a bed that conforms to your body almost as comfortably as a waterbed. You can even pile it up around the edges of your tent or fly to keep out the wind.

But almost as much as water, sand loves to get into your things. It can make your clothes itchy, and even worse, make your food very crunchy. If you don't like fingernails on a blackboard, just wait until you bite into a sandy sandwich. So it is important to be as vigilant against sand as against water. Keep things in plastic bags, and keep the plastic bags closed, even if they are inside a good tent.

Another potential horror is bugs. Now, you won't always have bugs. I have been camping many times and been left completely alone. But usually bugs, and especially mosquitoes, seem to breed in wet places. So bring along a good bug repellent.

We have already covered the importance of keeping your things dry. But sometimes they will get wet. Plastic bags puncture. Or the ties come off. Or something that shouldn't happen does happen. Then, it seems to me, there are two routes open to you. You can dry your things out, or you can live with them. Synthetics dry faster, so you will probably want to wear mostly synthetics. And wool keeps you warm even when it is wet, as do certain synthetic pile materials. Your wardrobe should include both types of fabric. Then, if you can't get dry, at least you can stay warm.

In my experience, the camper/cruiser is likely to be very punctilious about keeping things dry on the water, but is likely to relax a little once he gets ashore. This is especially true if it is a nice, warm, clear day. But it's important to remember that it may rain at night. More than likely, there will be some dew. I have known people to take off their clothes and scatter them around on the ground to dry out if they are damp, or to air out if they are a little ripe. They turn in for the night, and wake up the next day to soaking wet clothing. All it takes is an average night of dew. Keep things in your tent, or in closed plastic bags outside if there is no room in the tent. Even in your tent, it might be smart to keep things in plastic. You may get a storm —even a bad enough storm to blow your tent away.

Unless I know I'm going to be sleeping on fine dry sand every night, I like to have an air mattress or an Ensolite pad to sleep on. After bouncing around on the hard deck of a Sunfish all day, I don't want to massage my bruised hip bones and spine with pebbles and sticks. A sleeping bag is lighter and more comfortable than a blanket roll. And I find that a small pillow does wonders to insure a restful night. For me, it is worth the extra space it takes up, even on a Sunfish.

For shelter, I have used the Sunfish sail, a plastic tube tent, and a two-man nylon pup tent. I was worried that I was stretching the sail when I used it as a tent. The plastic tube tent often sweated inside, and, since it doesn't breathe, it can get stuffy. The light nylon tent, I have found, is the ideal solution. Again, it takes up some room, but it's worth it.

After a long day of sailing, I have found that it is very difficult not to like almost any kind of food. I don't need a gourmet meal. And anyway, who wants to spend hours cooking after hours on the water? I'm tired. So I make it as easy as possible, with things that are easy to cook and require a minimum of clean-up afterwards.

This is not a book on camping; it's a book on sailing. But most smart-camping practices are smart-camping/cruising practices. I mean the back-packing kind of camping, not the small house on wheels you plug in at a campsite. So I usually take along nothing but freeze-dried foods and things that come in relatively soft packages. I've been surprised at how many of these are available in the ordinary grocery store. You don't have to go and buy the super-expensive stuff at stores that sell camping equipment. Most supermarkets sell freeze-dried soups and one-step meals that you can make by pouring boiling water right into the bowl that is part of the package. There are dried fruits, nuts, and even powdered milk and lemonade. With one pot in which to boil water, and a folding sterno stove, you can have a different meal every night for a week.

I find that you can get along without canned goods and especially bottled drinks on a Sunfish cruise. They are heavy, they are uncomfortable to lie on, and they puncture plastic bags. Worst of all is bottled stuff. A cockpit full of broken glass is at best uncomfortable and at worst lethal. I find that a polyethylene gallon jug of drinking water will last me two or three days. Disposable plates, cups, forks and spoons, and a roll of paper towels completes the kitchen equipment.

Whether I am racing or cruising, I like to take along a basic tool kit in a plastic quart bottle. This consists of a pair of pliers, a regular and a Phillips screwdriver, two open-end wrenches that fit all the nuts on the Sunfish, a couple of shackles, a roll of waterproof tape, and about a 100-foot roll of strong nylon or cotton twine. I also carry a Victorinox Swiss officers' knife— I like the one with a saw blade and the little tweezers and toothpick. I have had very good luck with the Victorinox—even after constant soakings in salt water. It will occasionally get so stiff I break a fingernail trying to open it, and then I just soak it in very hot water for a while, followed by a very, very light spritz of WD-40 in the joints. But it really is rustproof, and a lot of so-called stainless steel things aren't. Most important, I must have a pair of scissors, the most useful tool of all. I think I use that three times for every time I use any other blade.

I always like to carry a bath-size Turkish towel when I cruise. A smaller one or even paper towels would do, but a big thirsty Turkish towel rub-down after a day of damp sailing renews my faith in the world.

As the world gets more and more crowded, it becomes more and more difficult to find campsites when you are camping/cruising. It makes sense to study the areas where you might spend the night, trying to find public campsites, obviously deserted areas, or very small islands that don't get submerged at high tide. Otherwise, make landfall early in the evening so that you can arrange to camp with the landowner's permission. I have never been refused, and have even been welcomed the following morning when I have not been able to get permission the night before. James Lee Meadows was welcomed wherever he landed, and he camp-cruised from Miami to Boston. But I suppose it is possible to be sent packing in the middle of the night by an irate landowner.

In summary, the most important things to remember about camping/cruising are to keep things dry, travel light, keep things dry, be prepared for cold and wet and bugs, and keep things dry.